THE CALL OF MUSIC

Praise for the book

'This is a rich and beautiful meditation on the greatest of our art forms. Herself an exceptionally gifted vocalist, Priya Purushothaman writes with elegance and empathy about the life and vocation of eight musicians of different backgrounds, whom she has known or studied with. While attentive to questions of caste, gender and religion, Priya never lets her focus waver from the "practice" of classical music, of what it means to devote oneself to learning, listening, absorbing, practising and performing. As a lover of our *shastriya sangeet* I found this book utterly compelling. So will readers with a more general interest in narrative non-fiction, and those seeking to make of their profession a calling.' – RAMACHANDRA GUHA

'Introducing readers to the lives, personalities, strengths, challenges, and music of eight artists who have inspired her over the years, Priya Purushothaman's writing reflects in totality the rigour and introspection that has marked her journey as a singer.' – SHUBHA MUDGAL

'*The Call of Music* is one of those rare books that forces us to see ourselves for who we are. In this collection of stories, Priya Purushothaman allows us to accompany musicians and learn from the intricate threads that stitch together their identity and life experience with making music. She brings together musicians from very different social and philosophical spaces and lets each of their stories flow into another, subtly initiating a conversation between them. This book is, in its essence, about finding and retaining one's own voice. For us, the readers, these are moments of personal reflection.' – T.M. KRISHNA

THE CALL OF MUSIC

8 STORIES OF HINDUSTANI MUSICIANS

PRIYA PURUSHOTHAMAN

hachette
INDIA

First published in 2025 by Hachette India
(Registered name: Hachette Book Publishing India Pvt. Ltd)
An Hachette UK company
www.hachetteindia.com

1

Front cover painting: 'Karnati Ragini, Folio from a Ragamala (Garland of Melodies)', via Wikimedia Commons
Cover design © Anna Thomas

Hardback ISBN 978-93-5731-507-4
eBook ISBN 978-93-5731-768-9

For sale in the Indian Subcontinent only.

Hachette Book Publishing India Pvt. Ltd
4th & 5th Floors, Corporate Centre,
Plot No. 94, Sector 44, Gurugram 122003, India

Typeset in Calluna 11/15.5
by R. Ajith Kumar, New Delhi

Printed and bound in India
by Thomson Press India Ltd.

MIX
Paper | Supporting responsible forestry
FSC® C010615
FSC
www.fsc.org

For my parents, Ramaa and Sampath,
for their unconditional love and support through
an unconventional journey

And for my uncle, Sundar, a tireless champion of the arts
and an emotional and intellectual anchor in my life

Contents

Introduction

THIS BOOK DOCUMENTS THE LIVED EXPERIENCES OF a group of Hindustani musicians who have deeply inspired me.

Music has been part of my life for as long as I can remember. As a toddler, I would sway along to M.S. Subbulakshmi inside my playpen as my mother cooked potent Tamilian delicacies that enveloped the house in aromas of asafoetida and fenugreek. Though I grew up in the verdant and relatively isolated suburbs of New York, I spent many summers in urban India, hopping in and out of neighbours' houses, eating chilli bhajjis on the beach, and always taking some form of music lessons. At the age of four, I remember the excitement of travelling with my grandmother by cycle rickshaw to attend her weekly *bhajan mandali* in Mylapore, Chennai. Back in my hometown, I had the great fortune of finding a Carnatic music teacher, Padma Subramaniam, who taught me meticulously, with grandmotherly affection. As I got older, I spent the summers attached to my aunt and uncle (Ranjani and Sampath Venimadhavan), Carnatic musicians who taught me various compositions: *thillana*s that became earworms, *kriti*s that bore gravitas, and eventually, *alapanai*, *kalpana swaram*, and *niraval* that introduced me to the thrill of improvisation.

And just as much as I wore out tapes of T.N. Seshagopalan by excessive re-listening, I idolized Itzhak Perlman and waited for my parents' monthly subscription to BMG music, a service through which I could order cassettes of my favourite violin concertos. My parents encouraged this interest from an early age, enrolling me in Western classical violin lessons at the age of five. While my first violin teacher indulged my inclination to burst into cartwheels during class, my primary teacher, Esther Slonczewski, later on taught me the importance of discipline and attention to detail. She was the first music teacher who made me feel like I had the quality of 'musicality' within me, some intangible ability to emote through sound. My soul was equally at ease in the competitive world of orchestras, chamber ensembles, and solo recitals that comprised this musical culture.

While these memories formed the backdrop to my musical life, the experiences that altered my core unravelled during my journey as a student and performer of Hindustani music. When I decided at the relatively late age of twenty-four to make a commitment to pursue this style of music as a profession, a blend of naïveté and idealism gave me the confidence to take the plunge. With time, I experienced the ups and downs – the frustrations and the small successes that dot the graph of an artistic career. But what kept me going, even when I felt overwhelmed by the sheer magnitude of the art form, were the inspirational musicians of Hindustani music whom I met along the way. Their stories, some heard and some unheard, form the contemporary landscape of this art. Whenever I encountered such individuals, I was reminded of the hardships and joys that artistes have endured purely for the sake of their art. These individuals often toiled in the shadows, and their moving journeys would reinvigorate me to stay on the path with a new perspective.

It goes without saying that the source of my inspiration starts with my gurus, with whom I have had deep musical and personal associations. I am aware that I stand on the shoulders of my entire guru *parampara* when I embark on a project like this. When I introduced myself to the musicians whom I wanted to interview, the first question they would ask me is: who is your guru? When I mentioned their names, I was immediately welcomed and trusted, though I was a complete stranger. This kind of acceptance and access is something I do not take for granted.

My gurus have shown me up close and unfiltered what it means to walk the path of *sadhana* in modern times. To be with your guru through moments of joy, loss, vulnerability, disagreement, and raw honesty, changes the way you make music. I believe this connection is destiny more than serendipity. I met my guru, Aditi Kaikini Upadhya, in 2002. My initial training with her was my first serious exposure to Hindustani music – until then, I had been a passive listener of select iconic Hindustani musicians. I connected with her so strongly that I came back to India after finishing my BA, living with her and her family to immerse myself into deeper study. I remember my grandfather telling me at the time how special it was for me to experience '*Gurukulavasam*' (training by living with the guru) – a system of study in artistic and spiritual practices that has become rarer these days. What was meant to be a one-year experiment expanded into two decades of living in India, where training occurred alongside performance.

Aditi Aunty, as I have always called her, possesses her own blend of modernity and tradition. The proportion of this blend was perhaps critical for our connection. Me, having been raised in New York, though my family had cultivated the *sanskar*s of classical music. She, coming from a family of distinguished musicians – her father being Agra gharana vocalist, Pandit Dinkar Kaikini. But she is also an individual who does not fear stepping outside of the weight of her legacy to embrace her own distinct identity. Her quality of boldness – as an individual and artiste – has always had a great impact on me. She has been a strong role model in my life.

Over the several years I lived with her, and the many years I trained with her while living in very close proximity, it goes without saying that I churned and churned in her *talim* (intensive training). She pushed me, never mincing words with her feedback, but always maintaining a critical balance of nurturing, support, and empathy. Aditi Aunty opened my eyes to the ways in which sound can be shaped, the necessity to have intentionality in each utterance, the layers of aesthetics embedded into a phrase, the thought process behind improvisation (both melodic and rhythmic), the strategic planning for performance, and the associated mental and physical preparation. And, of course, it goes without saying that she imparted a great deal of musical repertoire, the musical foundations upon which I stand today. *Riyaz karvana* means to get the student to do *riyaz* in front of the guru – it requires much patience, and it is often easier for the guru to leave it to the student to complete on their own time. I had the opportunity of going through this process with her. I would often wonder how many times she would listen as I sang the same raag over and over, at such a rudimentary level. I received this kind of exhaustive training in many raags, serving as a blueprint for my approach to those that followed.

Beyond music, what I also learned is that while *talim* forges forward at full pace, life also happens. *Talim* cannot occur in a bubble, as ideal as that would be. We do not always have control over the life circumstances that may arise during *talim* – but how do we respond without tremendous imbalance to our *sadhana*? My *talim* did not stop when Aditi Aunty underwent multiple surgeries. It did not stop when she had to care for her ailing mother-in-law. It did not stop when her family responsibilities mounted. She has shown me the balance of being a woman and being a musician. The question of feminism and classical music keeps recurring throughout my conversations with various artistes in this book – their roots certainly lie in my relationship with my guru. Watching her negotiate her gender in professional and personal contexts has been an essential part of the fabric that holds me together as I try to navigate my way forward.

My other guru, Sudhindra Bhaumik, is featured in great detail in this book. His life is cinematic in scope, filled with unbelievable obstacles, even more miraculous triumphs, and a crazed thirst for music. Bhaumikji's life is an example of the artistic spirit and living with unapologetic personal freedom. His story was one of the first that motivated me to create the collection, because I believe that so many people (artistes and non-artistes alike) could take inspiration from his radical approach to life.

During the pandemic, when the transiency of life took on an entirely new dimension, I felt an urgent need to document the inner stories of serious practitioners of music, some of whom are not in the limelight. If you're part of the music world, chances are that you've heard such stories through fellow musicians, perpetuating the casual culture of sharing oral histories that blur the boundaries between rumour, legend, and fact. I wondered about all the stories I wouldn't get to hear or read, out of sheer lack of access or documentation. This compelled me to seek these individuals and see if they would give me the privilege of sharing a slice of their lives, coming together as something akin to an ethnographic survey of select Hindustani musicians in the twenty-first century.

Normally, such collections would only feature senior artistes, senior by age, that is. I chose to include a spectrum of ages in this collection. Though the culture of Hindustani music glorifies age as a virtue – and certainly age often comes with wisdom and experience – I have also felt that this confines younger musicians to a permanent position of inadequacy. What a young artiste may lack in experience, they may compensate for in freshness of perspective. It is also not always the case that young artistes lack experience, because many musicians begin training at a very young age. By their thirties, they have been in the business for decades. I believe there is much value in hearing the thoughts of younger generation performers – to inspire other youngsters who may be looking up to them, and also to acknowledge that wisdom is not a function of time but of depth of experience and capacity for reflection.

The first musician featured, Alam Khan, reminds me of an old soul trapped in a young man's body. He is wise beyond his years, having immersed full time in this world since his teenage years. He carries the legacy of his father, Ustad Ali Akbar Khan, with tremendous humility, reverence, and responsibility. His deep commitment to musical honesty made me ponder the question of intention and awareness as we make music.

Shubhada Paradkar is an indomitable musical spirit whose music negotiates the lively spirit of the Agra and Gwalior gharanas, while challenging notions of gender in music.

Kala Ramnath's journey to becoming a world-renowned violinist is filled with a lifetime of consistent effort and a quest for a unique, individual voice by innovating on an instrument that was introduced quite late into the Hindustani music firmament.

Rumi Harish turns all conventions of Hindustani music upside down with his radical interrogation of concepts of gender and voice through his lived truths in music and activism.

The youngest musician in this collection is Suhail Yusuf Khan, a sarangi player who has performed around the globe, collaborated across genres, and become the first hereditary musician to earn a PhD in Ethnomusicology. Suhail opened my eyes to issues of caste and discrimination as a Mirasi musician.

Shubha Joshi has dedicated her lifetime to mastering the multitude of forms that comprise Hindustani music, deconstructing notions of the feminine voice while intentionally carving her own unique sound.

Yogesh Samsi speaks a complex language of tabla that has evolved through momentous historical moments of both loss and ingenuity. As a master soloist and accompanist, he shows the path to a future of aesthetic and intellectual music.

It is my hope that those who take the time to read this book will gain an insider's view into the creative processes of music making – the gruelling effort, dedication, and sacrifice that make a musician – as well as the undeniable presence of social issues in the world of classical music.

Often, musicians choose their path not out of choice, but from a persistent inner call, a driving necessity for their existence. Perhaps after reading these stories, you, the reader, will appreciate the complex life of a musician the next time you hear a piece of music or attend a concert.

A note on usage of certain terms:

The word raag appears very often throughout this book. Some artistes prefer using the word raga and others raag. Both terms refer to the same musical concept, the melodic framework of Indian classical music. I have retained each artiste's preferred usage in their direct quotes. In my own writing, I have adhered to the use of the word raag.

Non-English words have been spelled based on their colloquial use, however the glossary includes some of these terms with diacritical markings as a reference for their accurate pronunciations and more detailed explanations of their meanings.

1

ALAM KHAN

Legacy and Truth

DURING THE PEAK OF THE PANDEMIC, I WAS DOOMSCROLLING on Facebook when I came to a halt: Alam Khan was going live. In the Indian classical music world, this period saw an onslaught of social media content – a panicked response to the fear of 'losing relevance' in a world defined by constant attention and adulation. Alam Khan was an exception.

He offered an *alap* in raag Bhimpalashri as a panacea for the unprecedented levels of anxiety and stress the world was facing. 'When my father taught me this raag, he often described the feeling to be like animals in the forest gathering at sunset, tears welling up in their eyes as they say goodbye to each other and seek shelter for the night.' It was such a precise visual that felt so true – my relationship to a raag I had sung for many years was changed in that single sentence.

Amidst a blurry set of pandemic memories, this

moment is crystal clear – I experienced stillness, beauty, and deep sadness simultaneously. The image of this moment of vulnerability amongst creatures of nature, the unpretentious manner in which Alam shared the anecdote, and the music that followed – phrase after phrase of musical love – merged into a meditative twenty minutes in which I forgot the chaos spiralling outside.

In the words of his father, legendary sarod maestro Ali Akbar Khan, Alam is the chosen one. This could be viewed as the most coveted blessing or a curse of unimaginable pressure.

'I'm a messenger of my father, and I'm keeping the torch lit. For a lot of people, being the son of someone like him, if you do anything good, it's expected because you're your father's son, and if you do anything bad, it's your fault. Apple fell far from the tree. Yes, some of it is in the blood, but that's definitely not all of it by any means, because there are a lot of people with music in their blood who don't get it. I do have to recognize and acknowledge for myself the work that I have done, so I don't go into a dark place when things are not feeling good.'

When I speak to Alam, his quintessential Californian demeanour sometimes makes me forget his musical pedigree. Often in a hoodie, he is outwardly low-key and chill, inwardly intense and contemplative. He can be profoundly serious and at the same time incisively humorous. He is a being of paradox and dualities: tradition and modernity, legacy and individuality, east and west. But it is perhaps these paradoxes that root him in his deepest value: honesty. A set of core truths reside deeply within Alam Khan – these are his collective North Star, guiding decisions, musical or otherwise. Are there undeniable truths in Hindustani music, and when does music become dishonest?

—

'What's your name, Olive? Alan? I got asked that a lot growing up, and I still have to deal with that.'

Growing up in Marin County, California, in the 1980s, Alam inhabited two universes: the musical world at home and at the Ali Akbar College of Music, and the starkly American culture at school, and virtually anywhere else. While the South Bay is home to many people from the Indian diaspora, the North Bay is relatively less diverse. Often mistaken as Latino or Italian, Alam began negotiating his dual cultural background from an early age. 'I lived a pretty fragmented, partitioned life. I'm a mixed breed mongrel – nobody talks about being half white and half Indian. When I go to India, I'm looked at as a foreigner, and when I'm here in America, I'm looked at as Brown. Being brought up in the States as full Indian is very different from being half. I didn't really feel that there was anyone like me, so I just had to get comfortable in my own skin. I grew up more as an American kid – my culture was American.' He remembers listening to a lot of rap and grunge (his favourites were Nirvana, Soundgarden, Alice in Chains, and Pearl Jam, which he still enjoys), and being into sports and video games like most of his friends. His teachers and friends at school knew that his father was a famous musician from India, but his two worlds rarely intersected.

But it is also true that Alam had a deeply Indian experience at home, which was an alternate world governed by the culture of music. His father's room was filled from floor to ceiling with pictures of deities, much like the home of his grandfather, Maihar gharana founder, Acharya Baba Allauddin Khan. All religions were represented – pictures of Jesus, Buddha, Hindu deities, Guru Nanak, the Quran. When he asked his father what their religion was, the answer was always music. Khan Saheb's idea and practise of religion was largely tied to the idea of devotion and acknowledgement of a higher power from any religion. His daily practice included a personalized set of rituals that consecrated his space – pujas, reciting his Muslim prayers, changing the holy water, lighting incense, and praying to and believing in all of the gods.

The mystical power of these deities was a matter taken very seriously by Khan Saheb and his ancestors – what would be considered as myths were shared as facts, truths accepted without question. Stories about deities manifesting were common and numerous. Ma Saraswati visited the Maihar home late at night, dressed in a red sari, mysteriously disappearing through the wall when spotted by Alam's grandmother, Medina Begum. Coming from a lineage of Kali *sadhak*s, there were stories of gliding cobras with beards guarding Ali Akbar's room.

One time, an old woman asked a young Ali Akbar for help to reach her home, which was on a winding road far away on the other side of town. He agreed to help her, but knew that he would get home past his curfew and get severely scolded by his father. After they reached her home, she thanked him for his help and he turned around to find that he was back in front of his house. He believed Ma Sharada had visited him in human form. The retelling of these incidents added to a spiritual and mystical atmosphere in their California home. 'He always spoke the truth, so I believed it all. He would share an intense story, and then I would go to the store and get some ice cream,' Alam recounts, revealing the bizarre way in which such experiences co-existed with his otherwise normal American lifestyle.

Alam also spent large amounts of time at the Ali Akbar College of Music, the North American Hindustani music Mecca founded by Khan Saheb in 1967. The College, as most students call it, is situated in San Rafael and reverberates with the aura of a serious Indian gurukul. The student community is largely American, mixed with Indians and internationals, some spanning over several generations. A black and white picture of Khan Saheb hangs behind the stage, and his spiritual presence is palpable. From Khan Saheb's time, guru-shishya etiquette was maintained strictly, the protocols written on the wall. 'Never touch instrument with foot. Never walk over instrument. Never touch notebook with foot.' Inside the school, you might as well have been in India.

The College became an extended musical family that was part of Alam's formative years, the site of regular classes, concerts, and other celebrations. While attending concerts, Alam remembers playing and running around with the other kids, sometimes falling asleep during the *alap* and waking up when the *jhala* began. Social gatherings always featured delicious food – Khan Saheb was famous for his culinary skills. Often, the evening would lead to a large group of students sitting on the floor around Khan Saheb as he shared stories from his life.

'The Indian way was very much there. That's why I have so much of it in me. Other than speaking Indian languages, I grew up with a very Indian upbringing in a lot of ways, I really got both.'

And while the Bay was and continues to be his home, Alam's frequent visits to India played an important role in shaping his identity and nurturing his connections with his musical and familial roots. From the age of two, Alam travelled to India during the winter while his father went on tour around the country.

One of his earliest memories is of meeting his paternal grandmother, Medina Begum, in Maihar (Madhya Pradesh). Because she had lost her vision, she used her hands to feel her grandson's face and imagine what Ali Akbar's seventh son looked like. In return, Alam fed her hot jalebis and milk for breakfast. Though he continued to make visits to Maihar over the years, Alam spent more time based in Kolkata, with his mother Mary, brother Manik, and sister Madina.

Being surrounded by an immersive musical world, both in California and India, it gradually became inevitable that Alam too would explore a relationship with the sarod.

Despite the pressure of a lineage that spans across and within generations, Alam was never coerced into being a musician. At the age of seven, he received his first sarod, putting stickers in spots to mark the position of the notes. But his learning was on and off, sitting in group classes at the College and also receiving some one-on-one instruction from his father. At the time, his interest was in the music he heard on MTV, and his parents encouraged that by getting him an electric guitar. Sometimes Khan Saheb would peep in while he was playing, once in a while playing the guitar himself. Perhaps the rock inspired rebelliousness and anger of grunge felt planets away from meditative forays into raags, but certainly it was possible to love both, and Alam had the freedom to do so. 'My father never forced me to play sarod. There were a lot of periods when I thought, I don't know if I want to do this. He said, "I just want you to be happy and live your life, and if that means not playing sarod, then don't."'

It was his mother, Mary, who gently nudged him into a more formal learning routine, suggesting that she wanted his company to learn sarod in class at the College. They began by taking classes together and gradually Alam found himself completely immersed. He sat in on all the vocal and sarod classes, including the advanced classes that would initially go over his head. 'The whole class was flying, playing really long *taans* on the spot. I would sit there with them and watch them play – many times I couldn't keep up. I would be distraught afterwards and in tears, telling my mom that I can't do this, this is too hard. She would say, "The only difference here is between the people who give up and the people who don't. So, you don't have to do this, but if you do, you will get there. If you give up, you won't." So I didn't give up, and eventually I was the one playing everything in the class. I was playing it better.'

While Khan Saheb's influence looms large over Alam's persona, the unwavering emotional, musical, and practical support provided by his mother has given him the groundedness necessary to pursue an otherwise uncertain career path. When Alam speaks of difficult patches – musically or personally – it is Mary's advice that seems to cut through the noise with tremendous clarity and reason.

Mary Johnson was born in New York and grew up in Arizona and Los Angeles. She found her way to the world of Indian classical music in 1972 during the wave of the hippie movement. After hearing about a school in Northern California, with exceptional teachers of Indian music and dance, she boarded a bus at the age of fifteen, getting off in Marin County to meet a large group of people in their early twenties who had also arrived to learn various forms of Indian classical music. She began her studies in the North Indian classical dance form, *kathak*, with Pandit Chitresh Das. However, she soon switched to studying tabla with the visiting maestro, Ustad Alla Rakha. Her tutelage under him would continue for twenty years, following many guru-shishya protocols. Living in a West Marin community situated in a large forested area with the gurus and other students, she spent extensive time with Abbaji (as Ustad Alla Rakha was fondly called) and later with Ustad Zakir Hussain, training seriously to become a tabla performer. She supplemented her tabla lessons with vocal training from Khan Saheb. Over time, she realized that she did not want to be a performer. Love also blossomed between her and Khan Saheb, and the two decided to get married. Her tabla studies did not stop, however. For the past thirty years she has continued training under Pandit Swapan Chaudhuri. Her guiding presence in her childrens' lives (Alam has two full siblings, Manik and Madina), her critical leadership in the College as the director, and her silent unstinting support of Khan Saheb have established her as a pillar in the story of Alam's life.

'After my father got sick, it was because of her diligence and fighting to get the right treatments that he was able to live for all those other years. She held up the whole school and him by keeping all the operations going. The list goes on. She's just a fantastic woman. I think one of the things I got from her is that if you don't know how to do something, then you teach yourself and figure out how to do it.'

During Alam's formative years, Mary's support proved critical in an important childhood decision: to pull Alam out of mainstream schooling and enrol him in an independent study high school. By the time he was thirteen, Alam was immersed in *talim* and it became clear that he would benefit from the flexibility to tour and train with his father around the year, travelling around the US, Europe and India and taking his homework with him on the road. 'At the time I didn't really know if I wanted to be a touring musician for my whole life, but obviously I'm with my father and I'm learning, and this thing – my legacy and my life – I can't get away from that. If I did, I would feel like I'm turning my back on this. And I love the music, and music was the thing that I deeply connected with. I look at it now, and being a musician and artiste is really hard. It's a difficult life for sure. I don't know if I would have kept on pursuing music if I had done something different, so I choose to do this to whatever level I can and continue my family's legacy.'

Alam's *talim* continued to be a combination of sitting in his father's regular advanced sessions at the College, and lessons at home that were a bit more free-flowing in structure. Classes at the College would run in two-month-long sessions, during which Khan Saheb would select one or two raags and then compose the entire presentation: *alap, jhala, gat, vistar,* and *taans*. These renditions were taught and learned in their entirety as fixed compositions, meticulously and aesthetically crafted like any Western classical masterpiece. While Hindustani music is largely considered to be an improvised art form, Alam raises the important question: what is truly improvised? What portion of a performance can an artist claim is truly creative or original? For students, the process of replicating an entire raag presentation becomes an important step that instils raag information and aesthetics. But beyond being a teaching tool, Alam believes that these presentations could also be treated as pieces of composed music, credited and performed, creating another avenue in which Hindustani music can be practised and sustained. 'For instance, Ali Akbar Khan's 1972 Darbari Kanada is incredible. Someone can go on tour playing these compositions, and people can recognize them, just like you recognize symphonies.' The idea of crystallizing music like this is a very radical concept in the Hindustani world, where artists glorify the notion of spontaneous creation despite the fact that portions of many presentations are carefully crafted and rehearsed.

As Alam's training and involvement intensified, he was practising six hours a day, covering technique for scales such as *murchana*s and *alankar*s, and then mastering these fixed compositions. 'I would try to memorize these compositions, which is incredibly hard because it's like telling someone to memorize all of Beethoven, Bach and Mozart's repertoire without any sheet music. But it's just a matter of time and immersion in something. There's really no shortcut.'

Alam is characteristically candid on this matter, even in the public domain. At a concert in Delhi in 2022, while crediting his father as the composer of the *gat*s he presented, he tells the audience that his first solo concert was a completely set presentation. In his typical self-deprecating manner, he says, 'I don't know what's better, all the fixed lines or my own lines.' The concert he was referring to was his fourteen-year-old debut, in which Khan Saheb introduced him to the music world at the acclaimed Dover Lane Festival in Kolkata. With Pandit Swapan Chaudhuri on tabla, Alam played raag Zila Kafi, which he had been training to present verbatim from *alap* to *jhala*. He continued this approach for his first few performances, after which he went into a mix of recollection and recreation, and finally into a place of complete improvisation, sometimes modifying the *gat*s as well. 'That's another part of my father's style – he would not stick to the *gat* in one way. In the class, he would say, "Play it exactly the way I'm teaching it. I know you're going to change it on your own when you're out of the class."'

In his individual lessons with his father, Alam delved further into raag intricacies. While teaching *alap*, Khan Saheb followed the traditional pedagogical format in which the student follows and repeats after the guru until the raag phraseology is gradually internalized. Here too, Alam applied the same approach. '*Alap* to me was the most important, potent aspect of my training, because that's where I would get a real picture of the raga. I would memorize the *alap* like a composition. He would teach it to me for twenty minutes, I'd try to memorize the whole thing. If I could, I'd memorize the first five to ten minutes, then I'd do it with another lesson, and another lesson. Each one of these things is a new thing for me to memorize. And then, I'd take a line or idea from another lesson and put that with the *alap*, and eventually I'd forget which particular lesson these phrases came from.'

One of Alam's musical truths is the need for firm adherence to the raag as it was taught to him. Using numerous compositions to excavate all the data of a raag's identity and feel, he aims for precise and aesthetic execution of raag phraseology. 'The whole point of playing these lines is to play it like your teacher taught it, because that's the way the raga goes. Everyone's like, be original. With what? The raga? It has its own main lines, and it's really important how you do it – I'm going to do it the way it was taught. I don't know if there's a question of being original here.'

Alam uses the metaphor of navigating the map of a city as his way of unfolding a raag. Just as a city is identified by its recognizable landmarks, parks, and main streets, a raag is characterized by its landmark phrases. It is up to the traveller to decide how to get from one point to another, how long she wants to spend travelling, and what her final destination will be. The path of journeying between these immovable structures is a personal and creative choice.

Deep listening is a critical faculty in the process of raag assimilation. In a mimetic learning system, the rate of a student's progress is directly proportional to the amount of information perceived while listening to the guru. On the first listen, it may just be notes and phrases. On the second repetition, perhaps more attention is paid to the rhythm or cadence of the phrase. For the third time (if the guru indulges), the student may observe tone, texture, feeling. The raag expression lives in the sedimented layers of detail behind each note, each phrase. Thus, training of the ear is equally important to the mastery of the instrument.

'I tell my students, when you think you've listened as closely as you can, listen closer. Because you are missing something. And when you get to the point when you're not missing anymore, *then* you've got all the information. Then you can really control that ship and guide it how you want, because it's about the follow through of what you're doing. You listen to these master musicians who play or sing, when they say something, they mean it. There's so much information in that line that they're doing, and there's so much weight in it. When you hear other people, their playing can be really sugary – it's sweet, but it gives you a toothache and you have a cavity after too many minutes. Where's the weight, where's the depth?'

And while most musicians spend decades toiling to hone that ability to musically converse in a raag, it may also be true that raags operate at a spiritual and mystical level. The student must surrender to the will of the raag, following it in pure form. Under these conditions, perhaps 'the goddess will smile upon you, inspire you, and the raga will show its face to you. Go in first with the mentality of treating the raga with respect, devotion, and humility. Then the rest will come,' Khan Saheb told Alam. It is widely known that Khan Saheb was a strict follower of the raag time cycle, never playing a raag (even during practice) out of its prescribed time window. Similarly, his legendary anecdotes about certain raags made these ethereal feelings floating in the air more tangible, sometimes associated with superstition and supernatural power. Puriya is like poison, only to be taken in small doses. Marwa is akin to being lost in the desert during dusk. Deepak, the raag of fire, must be played far away from people. Ghostlike genies emerge upon hearing Malkauns – if played correctly, they grant wishes, but if played incorrectly, beware. When one student at the College played Yaman at the wrong time and a tree fell on his car that day, students took heed to follow the raag time cycle, else they were told their families would be cursed.

Beyond the spooky and magical, Khan Saheb of course dove into the nitty-gritty of raag complexities, sharing the subtleties of *andolan* and *shruti* with Alam and the group classes. *Andolan*, a very specific oscillating movement between notes with careful use of *shruti* (microtones), is one of the subtle effects that enables raag penetration. Often, he would demonstrate differences in the commercial or mainstream treatment of such nuances (even in his own public releases) as compared to a more nuanced approach for refined ears.

'He'd talk about *andolan* a lot. He would sometimes show me the *andolan* for Shree, Darbari, these kinds of ragas with *komal*, *ati komal*, *ati ati komal*, and the movement of these microtones. It was so hard to get, because it wasn't just moving in one direction, like a slow *gamak*. It would reverse at times, sometimes midway, creating an illusion of what was going on. But then you would hear him play in certain recordings or concerts where he didn't play it that way. He gave a more generalized vibrato. He would say, "This is the general *andolan* on *komal ga* which is going to be pleasant to hear and has movement," but I know that if he taught it to me, he would only sometimes play it like that – he taught it to me in a different way. He would often say this is the way we do this line, and this is the commercial way. He would make that distinction a lot.'

Khan Saheb grew stricter as Alam's *talim* intensified. Whether in the group lessons at the College or at home, he would express his dissatisfaction with specificity. 'This is out of tune, this is not the right feeling here, that's not the way the rhythm goes with that ornament, keep working on it. There's no life in that, no feeling,' Alam remembers him saying. 'When it got to a certain point, if it wasn't something that could be described in terms of timing or intonation, it would go back to the feeling. You're not bringing feeling. Sometimes he would give examples: this sound is the feeling of your love for your mother or father.' To illustrate dynamic range, he would demonstrate how human expression varies with tone and volume as used in speech patterns.

Deeply immersed in his father's training, Alam never felt the need to look elsewhere for additional guidance or another perspective. But, if ever there was anyone else Khan Saheb felt he should learn from, it was his sister, Vidushi Annapurna Devi. It is widely known that she faced great adversity in her life, living many years in solitude. However, this did not diminish her *sadhana*, devotion and adherence to her father's musical teachings. On Alam's trips to India, he would visit her whenever he was in Mumbai. Once, while visiting with his family, he remembers playing raag Bilaskhani Todi for her – but it was only when he was alone with her, without his father, that she would teach him. She would openly admit that her approach and Khan Saheb's could differ – as a performer for the public whose imagination could not be contained, Khan Saheb explored the raag in ways that were different from her. When Alam shared some of her corrections with his father, his reply was, 'That's not the way I learnt it.' The question of truth in music again surfaces – could there be multiplicity of truths in a raag? 'In this situation maybe you really don't know. Maybe Baba did learn it that way and she didn't learn it that way. At some point you also have to trust that it is subjective and each person is learning something differently.'

Interestingly, though she was a recluse, Annapurnaji was observing the popular trends in instrumental music and advised Alam to explore more usage of *taan*s in his renditions. 'Unlike me, you perform for audiences, and nowadays they like to hear certain things,' he recalls her telling him. She taught Alam a series of simple exercises that are nonetheless very challenging to execute: *ekhara*, *dara,* and *sapat taan*s, essentially extensive scale work.

Though Khan Saheb also taught Alam these *taan* varieties, he was less inclined to perform these in concert. Alam too is not greatly interested in the idea of prioritizing speed or *taans* in his overall presentation. 'I practiced that for years and got to a certain point where I realized this is not really where I excel in my playing. I know that there are others who can do it much better. But I heard her, and I try to incorporate different things. So, I do it to a point, to show that this is an aspect of the music that is beautiful, but I don't get lost in that.'

His time with Annapurnaji, though limited, left him with strong memories of a 'very sweet, small, unassuming and powerful woman,' whom he made laugh a lot. 'I wish I could have spent more time with her,' he remembers wistfully.

'When we're on stage, it all goes out the window.'

There were two sides of Alam's music education: in the classroom and out on stage. His exposure to performance began from his early teens, when he would accompany his father on tours in Europe and India as well as across the US. Life on the road had a different rhythm: constant changes of location and pace while trying to maintain a sense of calm, routine, and normalcy. Alam shadowed his father's routine, gradually performing many of the tasks expected in a typical guru-shishya relationship.

For Khan Saheb, perfection and attention to detail

were not only musical standards: they were a way of life. Punctuality, preparation of tea and food, ironing of clothes. 'If I didn't do these properly, he would be hard on me. I kept a lot of urgency and anxiety around getting things done, which I still do as an adult. I remember that being stressful, I can still see myself thinking of things like that, although I try to ease up on it because it makes me anxious. But, if that's the worst of it, then it's not terrible. For him, it was just this sense of "how are you going to do the music if you can't treat these things with a lot of care?"'

A typical concert day for Khan Saheb was quiet, avoiding unnecessary disturbance. Following a timely schedule of eating and resting, Khan Saheb would do a small puja, recite his prayers, and reach the venue very early. On stage, the spirit of performance took over: it was a time to take risks and break free. There were no safety nets or sticking to comfort zones.

'He told me, "Lions don't teach their cubs in the den, they teach them in the jungle. That's what the stage is." He showed me how to take that dive. You're going on an adventure, and you don't know what it's going to be – that's why his music feels like a journey.'

In improvised music, risk taking is where spontaneity, presence, and imagination thrive. With countless hours of preparation, an improvised musician can recreate what was practiced at home on stage, but is that truly improvisation? On stage, skill, knowledge, and mastery become the mechanisms to break free from structure or expectation.

Diving into this zone on stage requires supreme levels of confidence, a validation that doesn't come easily or often from guru to shishya. The tradition has a reputation of keeping students in a permanent place of modesty, a quality that may be valuable for self-reflection and growth, but which can hinder fearless freedom on stage. 'They're [gurus] always holding you down in a way to keep you humble for how big and vast the experience is going to be in your life. Because they've experienced that too. I think it's a fine line between following your teachers in that way, and maintaining confidence. For me, Baba would support me enough but he was also very critical – I took it very personally and wanted to get what he was saying, so I was really hard on myself, which made me sometimes scared to try things. Because you don't have the confidence. Being able to find that balance between confidence and humility is a pretty tricky one. I've worked on that for a long time and I still do work on it. Sometimes when you say to hell with it and let loose, that is when you make your biggest growth. Just go for it, take a dive. But believe in yourself and be confident.' On stage, a mere look or a smile from his father would indicate that Alam had done something right.

And while performance, at some level, is an exchange of energy with the audience, there are artists, like Khan Saheb and Alam, for whom the art comes first, the audience second. Concerts of Khan Saheb, and now Alam, have minimal visual distractions. Their eyes are usually closed, head down, with the occasional acknowledgment of their co-artistes. A dramatic hand gesture is very rare, perhaps only at the end of an entire raag presentation. In the modern age of showy interactions with audiences, this demeanour could be construed as aloof. But, for Alam, it again comes back to authenticity and truth.

'My father was like a shaman, communing with the cosmos, being a conduit. We're all sitting in the audience, watching him in this experience and having our own transformative experience. My father wasn't an entertainer, he was honest. Entertainers are not always honest, they are contrived, doing things to get a reaction. My father played exactly what he was feeling in that moment, the audience could be there or not. It was just honesty.'

In the current scenario, in which many artistes seek large numbers of followers on social media to build their audiences, it seems that they may not have the luxury of creating art in a rarefied bubble. Those who choose not to may pay a price, a price to retain their musical integrity. Or, perhaps there is a middle road.

'I try to find a balance between entertainment and the transformative, spiritual way of looking at the music. Sure, we all like being on stage, and we all like when audiences like the music. But that is not behind the wheel for me. I care about my own creative spirit. I feel like a lot of people are more about the audience these days.'

What is *your* sound?

This is a question that Alam faces often – to some, it is not sufficient to recreate the effect of his father. Critics ask, what is Alam's voice, what is his musical identity?

'That's the voice my father gave me, and that's why I try to speak with his voice on the sarod. I don't want to change any tone I have because I spent many years trying to recreate that tone. It has all the information and soul in it. To me that is the most refined sound on an instrument. It's like the sound of unconditional love. If you have unconditional love, there's nothing more. Speak with that voice, sing with that voice, play with that tone. That's the sound, man!'

The aesthetics of that sound is built upon layers of thought, experimentation, and most importantly, the humanization of music. Distilling and channelling life's experiences, whether lived or not, into musical form. In Khan Saheb's varied life, this is perhaps most informed by the severity of his upbringing. Often told to sleep fully clothed with his sarod tuned and ready right next to his bed, his father would call him in the middle of the night to play. If he didn't respond after being called three times, he would be scolded or beaten. The musical path did not allow for a normal childhood, or any childhood for that matter. He tried to catch a few moments to read detective books, his favourite genre, by the moonlight. And to escape from his father's militaristic regimen, he would often be found in the kitchen with his mother, perhaps where he developed his love for cooking. But what he sought the most, a moment of softness or acknowledgment from his father, was rarely received, and if so, only in the context of music.

'He didn't get to look at my grandfather's eyes in his life because his head was always down, but he knew that his father loved him very much. It's really heart wrenching because he was just a little boy who wanted to be loved and given love by his father. And his father didn't show that to him in that way. He showed it to him through music – he wanted my father to take all of the years of pain and his sacrifice to become who he was. My father showed me that this brutal militaristic upbringing crafted one of the finest musicians this world has ever known. Something worked from that, but at the expense of the psychological damage that would be considered quite abusive and traumatic. We use that word so easily now – despite the trauma my father had, he lived a long life and was a very put-together gentle, sweet, loving person. He channelled it all into his music. Perhaps that is the reason he had the dynamic and human range of his experience in his music. He used to say, "When I play my instrument, I weep inside, I cry within my music and you can hear that." You can hear that pain when he's playing. You can see the whole experience of life.'

Though Alam's childhood was vastly different from his father's, his life of over forty years now has already been filled with his own share of emotional learnings. Like his father, he is a man of moods and deep feelings, and this quality translates into his music as well.

'I feel like you have to really allow yourself to feel very deeply about things in normal life. And if you want to touch that place in music, for me, you have to experience it. I'm someone who has always been controlled by my emotions rather than being in control of them, for better or worse. It's taken me to very high and low places. When I'm playing, the powerful emotional feelings come from an experience in life. If you're shut off, you're not going to feel a whole lot. Some musicians may be very scientific about stuff, and there's nothing wrong with that, but they might be like doctors that have no bedside manners. At the end of the day, I relate to the tones, the feelings. Even just the slide between two notes can unlock a lot. And Baba could do that really well. When you heard a line like that, it went right to the soul. There is everything in that one phrase. That to me sums up all of life and the human experience. That's what I try to go for, trying to chase after that feeling. You can't teach feeling, you can show by example. The student has to go there himself.'

The quest for his distinct and fresh voice – free of comparison and expectation that he faces in the classical realm – emerges in his collaborative music endeavours. The structures of Hindustani music do not create an unconstrained canvas for pure sonic exploration. In his personal projects, Alam's interest lies in aesthetically bringing the sound of the sarod into different contexts. He is very clear that his work does not fall into the category of fusion, a term that he strongly dislikes for its reputation and lazy categorization of anything non-classical. 'These terms are very important in today's world. And when you use that label, there are connotations behind the music – I'm not going to be lumped in with that guy. Hell no. Your fusion thing is not the same as my fusion thing. I generally dislike most fusion bands. When I'm making something, I am not trying to make fusion music. I am trying to express my creative spirit with all the things I like. My father used to say about fusion music: "is it fusion or confusion?"'

His strong stance on the issue refers to the mix and match of musicians of different genres together, often for the sake of novelty. Ironically, this has become so common that there is no novelty left in such endeavours. True collaboration, in Alam's view, involves thoughtful, aesthetic, and studied approaches to all the music forms involved, from instrumentation and arrangement to album artwork and titles. It is not ad-hoc. It is not the product of a jam session. It is a considered, detail-oriented, creative process. The sarod – as an instrument – is at the centre of these explorations.

In this space, Alam finds a space to draw upon the many musical and cultural influences in the spectrum of his life. 'It's about being authentic, taking elements that were my honest experience – from listening to hip hop, grunge, rock, electronic, Indian classical – and creating from that space. For a long time, I kept these two separate, and I was in between them. Eventually I just found my own world between these worlds. I tried to create from that unique space, and that's me. That's the sound of my life. I feel like I'm making something that has integrity, that is very artistic, fresh and unique to me. That is what matters to me when I'm making music outside of Indian classical. Here, I can be free of everything and express my creative spirit to the farthest reaches that makes sense for playing sarod in something. I can be free of the structure of Indian classical music.'

Alam's collaborations are based on in-depth research and understanding of the genres and artists he works with: Eligh, the Los Angeles rapper/producer; Tedeschi Trucks Band, a blues and rock group; the Del Sol Quartet and Blake Mills. He has also composed music for film and dance, as he is interested in cinematic music that is inspired by visuals. His album, *Mantram*, was commissioned for a dance production by the Chitresh Das Institute.

Ultimately, the search for expression circles back to the question of individuality in tradition.

'Tradition can be such a handicap for us – we have to work within this world that can at times feel so limiting. We're expected to have our own style in a super traditional world. I can't jump over this building right now, I'm in the alleyway of this complex network and I can't reinvent the wheel. When you're doing other music – like a producer, rapper, or band – they're just going with it, anything that hits their mind. Whatever they make is theirs. It's not based on tradition, so they have that freedom to create. And I want to be able to make music that's mine, in that sense. It's my story that I am trying to tell.

'My story in Indian music is also my father's and grandfather's and Tansen's and everybody else's story too. We're continuing it, but we like to think we're so individual. But, it's very connected to other people and traditions. It's amazing – I love Indian classical music. It's my lighthouse, my guiding light. But, when we're talking about just being creative, I feel like it doesn't give me enough creative freedom to pour everything into.

'The thing that I love about classical raga music is that it takes you to different places. To states of sorrow, happiness, wonder, mystique, enchantment, detachment, all these things, but then it returns you back to a baseline *sa*. It resolves itself emotionally. Where you listen to a song that is so sad, it only gives you that. Indian music takes you through the experience and then resolves itself to a place of tranquillity and peace, and that's something that's really special about Indian music. These other music forms, even other stuff that I make, don't necessarily resolve all the time.

'These types of music present a chapter. In Indian music, the whole thing is a story and you're creating it every time.'

Since his father's passing in 2009, Alam has taken over the role of Director of Instrumental Music at the College. His mission of 'keeping the torch lit' drives his commitment to teaching. Thanks to his mother's meticulous and persistent efforts in the field of archival studies, the College now has an exhaustive audio and notated archive of Khan Saheb's entire teaching repertoire spanning a forty-year period. Alam and his siblings, as well as students, invested countless hours in digitizing DAT (Digital Audio Tape) and cassette formats, scanning notations and cataloguing – some students even quit their jobs to work exclusively on completing the archive.

Alam is very clear about how the archive is meant to be used. It will not be accessible to the public online – anyone who is willing to physically visit the college will be allowed to browse the material. No recording or photos will be allowed. In the current age of effortless access to information, Alam is particular that knowledge housed in the archive is valued with the respect and commitment of in-person *talim*.

'You have to sit there and spend time learning the compositions. Not just grabbing that one and this one – that is not the appropriate thing to be doing here. You need to be sitting, learning. Immediate access, like we have for so many things in this internet age, is not something that should be applied to Indian classical music, otherwise it's never going to be grasped in the way it should. You have to have someone physically guiding you – so we always say, access the archive and take classes with a physical person. Doing these things together will form a huge picture, at least for learning in the Ali Akbar Khan Maihar style of music. But you can't take a photo of it, and you can't record it, and we're not putting it online. It's like putting out all your jewels, which are now worth a penny each.'

When Alam was born, his father was already sixty years old. He faced the unusual predicament of knowing that the time he had with his father would be relatively less than a typical father-child lifespan. Coupled with the pressure to acquire knowledge from him that is inherently slow to assimilate, Alam jostled between being a regular kid and trying his best to be a serious shishya. In his later years, Khan Saheb struggled with a serious kidney ailment, and despite extensive efforts to support him, the family knew his end was approaching.

'He would say to me before he died, "You're still a baby in this." I asked him, what am I going to do without you? He would say, "You have all my recordings, all the lessons. Keep learning from that. I've showed you everything technique-wise on the instrument, and you're doing everything that I was showing. You need to keep learning from all of that," and that's what I do. I think about it all the time, I have so many questions, which I knew I would. I tried to ask what I could at that time, but of course there's not enough time and you don't have all the questions to ask because the questions arise later. There's always going to be more.'

At Khan Saheb's funeral, it was again raag Bhimpalashri that was a balm of sorts, managing to console, evoke, and remind of beauty even in deep sorrow. Family and students gathered to pay respects, congregating around a giant redwood tree atop a lone hill where Khan Saheb was buried. They listened in silence as Khan Saheb's *alap* reverberated through speakers, his spirit and music in communion with all the living elements of nature.

For Alam, underneath layers of grief and loss remained the solid bedrock of his musical heritage. The way forward was clear. He returned to his instrument, making the music that spoke his truth.

2

SHUBHADA PARADKAR

Fate and Perseverance

DURING AN OTHERWISE TYPICAL MORNING, FILLED WITH the repetitive rituals of making chai, planning meals for the day, and easing into the tasks that lie ahead, the Paradkar household in Dombivli (suburban Mumbai) received an unexpected visitor at 6.30 a.m. Despite the abnormally early time to drop in unannounced, the guest was exceptionally brisk and alert. He stood in an erect and commanding posture. '*Mi* Gajanan Joshi,' he declared in Marathi.

The elderly lady of the house recognized the man and immediately invited him inside. He was the musician who lived in the neighbourhood, often spotted during his morning and evening walks from her veranda. But what could he want at this hour, what was the urgency of the visit? She immediately rushed in and woke up her son, Satish. 'Gajanan Joshi has come! Gajanan Joshi has come!' she exclaimed, and he immediately bounced out of bed, freshened up and went outside to greet him.

After exchanging customary greetings, Gajananbua (as he was fondly called), hastened to the point. 'Who sings in this house?' he asked Satish.

'My wife Shubhada sings, but she is not at home right now,' Satish explained. 'She's at her mother's house in Baroda because we just had a baby daughter ten days ago.' It was still unclear what Bua wanted, but Satish was intrigued at his sudden appearance and interest in his wife. 'But how do you know of her?' he dared to ask.

Gajananbua then shared the story of how he received a six paise inland postcard from a dear friend and music lover who heard Shubhadaji sing in a local programme. The friend had urged him to hear this promising young singer who lived in his own neighbourhood, a Dombivli of the 1960s that was far removed from the hustle of Mumbai, filled with greenery and a local community of diehard Hindustani music fans. For Gajananbua, a towering musician and all-consuming musical thinker, it was hard to imagine that he was unaware of a talent in his community.

Satish was no stranger to music, though he was a statistician by profession. He understood very well the import of this moment. In fact, soon after he married Shubhadaji, he made many attempts to find her a guru in Mumbai. From Dombivli to Dadar and beyond, he embarked on a search for the right mentor for his wife. The first stop on this search six months earlier was in fact at Bua's home, but luck had it that Bua was in Nashik. Some students who were staying at his house at the time spoke on his behalf and declared that he was not taking any new students. A disappointed Satish accepted this fate and left, continuing to search for her guru elsewhere.

When Satish recounted this incident to him, Bua laughed. And then he proceeded to encourage the family to bring Shubhada back to Mumbai as soon as possible so he could start teaching her. As far as he was concerned, the fact that she had just given birth to her first child was merely a detail in the larger spectrum of her musical growth.

Shubhadaji remembers this moment well. 'We didn't have a phone at the time at my parents' home in Baroda. Two to three days later, I received a letter from my husband. He described how Gajananbua had come to our house looking for me – he felt that it was good luck brought by our daughter, Rashmi. Then he asked me to finish the namkaran (naming ceremony) immediately and come back as soon as possible. I was so happy, so much so that I didn't think about whether I needed more rest or time after the delivery. My mother and grandmother also didn't ask me to stay back or rest – they were so thrilled that Gajananbua had agreed to teach me! So just a fortnight after my baby's birth, I finished the naming ceremony and left that very night by train to Mumbai.'

While many stories surrounding the guru-shishya relationship portray the shishya as a seeker at the whims of the guru's temperament, there are also stories like Shubhadaji's that serve as a reminder that more unconventional narratives also exist. How often does a guru show up at the doorstep of the shishya, insisting that *she* learn from *him*?

Shubhadaji was anxious about her first lesson with Bua – she hadn't sung in the past two months. She was worried about the state of her voice and mind. What would she sing for him in their first encounter? But all her worries seemed irrelevant after meeting him; Bua did not even feel the need to hear and evaluate her. He knew and respected her previous guru, Madhusudan Joshi, an Agra gharana vocalist from Baroda. 'Bring the tanpura and sit,' he told her, not wasting time on any formalities. Shubhadaji, however, had practical concerns – would she be able to afford the class fees? Her husband was the sole earner at the time, and she wanted to make sure the fees wouldn't add undue financial stress on the family. But such topics were not to be discussed; it was music and music only, and soon after taking the tanpura, Bua started off her *talim* with a rare and difficult raag, Gara Kanada. In addition to grasping an unusual raag, Shubhadaji was also adjusting to an entirely new *gayaki* that operated in largely *madhya laya* (medium tempo) movements.

'That day I thought to myself, how will I ever get this music?' she remembers. But Bua ended the class by saying, 'Come tomorrow and continue to come every day.' She went home and shared the news, and to her advantage, she had the practical and emotional support of her husband's family as she navigated this new phase of life that juggled children, family responsibilities, and in-depth *talim*.

She would wake up early and help her mother-in-law

prepare for the day in the kitchen. In between these tasks, she would feed her newborn daughter Rashmi every hour and half, trying to understand her moods and ensure that she was getting the care and attention she needed. No matter what, she had to reach Bua's house with utmost punctuality for her *talim* as he was an absolute stickler for time.

The first six to seven months of her *talim* proceeded in this fashion, and even if baby Rashmi was crying when she left, Shubhadaji would leave her with her mother-in-law and reach Bua's house on time. After one and a half hours (or sometimes longer), she would rush back home to feed her, after which she would again help with cooking and household tasks that were pending.

Initially, Shubhada's *talim* was a mixture of individual classes and a women's group class. With time, her sincerity and commitment became evident. While the others in the women's batch gradually faded away, Shubhadaji remained steadfast and mustered the courage to ask Bua if she could attend the lessons of another senior student, Ulhas Kashalkar. He readily agreed, and within an instant, her time with him doubled and she was again in the position of making time for music amidst the multiple responsibilities of home life.

Classes with Ulhasji began at 9 a.m. sharp, but if for some reason he was late, Bua would ask Shubhadaji to start singing and the lesson would become hers. When they were together, they would alternate between singing and listening, both paying close attention to whatever he was imparting. Shubhadaji continued to attend her individual afternoon slot, except now Ulhasji would attend that session as well. The two of them trained together for almost four hours every day without interruption: no weekends, no holidays, no festivals. None of these occasions warranted a break in Bua's eyes for the entire seven years Shubhadaji trained under him.

And when she transgressed, she would not be spared. 'Once during Dussehra, I missed one class, and he scolded me so much. When I told him that it was a festival day, he said that there are no holidays! I used to get so bored because I had just got married a year and half ago, moved to Mumbai, had a baby, and we never went around anywhere for fun – to Chowpatty, to the movies, just roaming around the city. But when I complained about this to my husband, he got so angry. "You're receiving such precious musical knowledge. Learn as much as you can." After that, I never said anything else on the matter.'

Bua's emotional investment in his students, musically and personally, was a remarkable quality that showed his deep concern and realistic understanding of the demands of a musical career. Two and half years into her *talim*, Shubhadaji gave birth to her second child, Ranjeet. After coming back from her mother's house in Baroda, Bua asked to meet her husband, Satish. In a private conversation, he spoke frankly and directly. '*Ata tumhi ithe thambaa* (Stop here.)' Do not have any more children, do not trouble her further. She has to sing.

While some would view this as a transgression into a very personal and private decision, Shubhadaji felt that such a statement only reinforced his commitment to her well-being, success, and fulfilment in a musical path. 'He worried and cared about his students in all aspects of their lives. *Kitni badi baat hai*.'

The *talim* itself was fast paced, packed with density of information and deeply entrenched in *gayaki*. The work of each day would depend on what raag was on Bua's mind. After introducing the raag phraseology, he would insist on a very clear understanding of the raag *swarup* (shape or form), *chalan* (phraseology and movement), and overall frame: its features and their movement. Microscopic attention to these details was essential to bring a raag to life. There was great emphasis on capturing the essence of the raag within the first few phrases, removing any similarities that may exist between neighbouring melodies. *Suron ka lagav*, or the approach to the utterance of each note, was critical in establishing the identity of the raag, and her training reinforced these ideas.

*Bandish*es formed the core framework, and because he did not allow any writing or notebooks in the class, Shubhadaji would rush home and write the compositions down immediately while her children glued themselves to her having missed her all morning. In each raag, he would teach her two to three *bada khayal*s, each with the *sam*, or first beat, landing on a different note. He emphasized the importance of having mastery over a variety of compositions, especially important in designing different types of performances. 'For a full concert, he would recommend choosing a *bandish* with a *sam* in the lower half of the scale, but for a shorter concert that is part of a larger lineup of artists, he suggested using a *bandish* that is *uttarang pradhan* (based in the upper half of the octave). If you have to sing after a good singer, you have to create your own impression, you have to change the mood. An *uttarang bandish* creates an immediate change. He taught us many such tactics about how to prepare for a concert, and how to choose and present *bandish*es like these that were composed in the higher part of the scale.'

Beyond the *bandish*, Bua's *talim* encouraged a free exploration, in which students would create a small impromptu *mukhda* within a taal cycle, exploring and circling around raag phrases in a musical dance.

Bua was known as a master of three storeyed gharanas: Gwalior, Jaipur, and Agra. His ability to connect to the stylistic elements of each, without allowing them to intermingle with each other, continues to be a highly celebrated aspect of his musicianship. While teaching, he insisted on the same discipline from his students, always pointing out the distinguishing elements and their musical sources. 'There was no mixing at all. He would keep singing to us and show us the flavour of the different styles. He would explain to us, "This is the Jaipur style, listen to Kesarbai. This is Mallikarjun Mansur. This is my father, Antubua. This is Nivruttibua, Rehmat Khan Saheb, Faiyaz Khan Saheb." This is how we would demonstrate the various styles. It also depended upon the raag – when he taught us Savani, it was pure Jaipur.'

In addition to gharana-centric learning, taal *kriya*, or training in all aspects of taal and *laya*, was critical in the internalization of the *gayaki*. Bua himself played the *dagga* (the larger bass drum of the tabla pair) while teaching all his classes, and would often encourage any young tabla player in the area to come for accompaniment. He would teach them lesser played taals like Tilwada and Jhumra, which feature prominently in Gwalior gharana *gayaki*. He also taught his students to play the *dagga* as they sang, ensuring that they developed an unshakeable grip over the *theka* that was rooted in the physicality of playing the instrument. In an effort to merge efficacy and expediency, Bua even taught Shubhadaji's husband the technique to play basic tabla syllables, urging him to accompany her at home during her *riyaz*. 'He understood that I was a girl from a middle-class family, and my husband was the sole earner. If I were to call someone for tabla *riyaz*, we would have to pay them per session. He was always looking out for me that way.'

Beyond the act of playing the tabla, Bua insisted that his students learn traditional tabla repertoire even though they were vocalists. Shubhadaji remembers learning and reciting various types of tabla compositions: almost 200 *qaidas*, *peshkar*, and *tukda* patterns upon his insistence. In a rare moment when she complained about lack of time to practise these in addition to her vocal *riyaz*, he came back with a quick solution. 'He told me to keep the book next to me while I was making rotis and keep practising them. There was no question of not having enough time.'

Following this advice as much as possible, Shubhadaji squeezed in time for *riyaz* early in the morning, followed by some housework, before which she hurried off for her lesson at 9 a.m. Rushing back home by 11, she would look after the children, feed them, and manage another period of practice before her 3.30 class. Before her husband came home in the evening, she would again manage to carve out some time if possible. Despite being a very hectic and taxing period of her life, she was immersed in music and *talim* and looks back on it as the 'golden days.'

—

It would be incomplete to tell the story of Shubhadaji's musical journey without the saga of her love story. In her case, music was both a commonality and a catalyst in bringing her together with her husband, Satish. Before their meeting, the seeds of music had been planted in each of their lives. This would lead to many fortuitous life events.

Born and brought up in Baroda in 1957, Shubhadaji's family was filled with music lovers, but no professional musicians. Her childhood musical memories are inspired by old Hindi film songs, Marathi *bhavgeet*, and many hours spent listening to All India Radio, trying to catch channels in Indore, Bhopal, Sangli, and Sri Lanka. Her formal training in classical music started late, by modern standards. Though she had been singing intuitively from a young age, she was fifteen when she began lessons in basic *palta*s and a few foundational gharanas. This made her pursue a diploma in music at the Baroda School of Fine Arts alongside her degree in commerce. During her college years, she studied with musicians of two different gharanas, Kirana and Agra. In private *talim* with R.D. Poddar, Shubhadaji imbibed distinguishing qualities of the Kirana gharana: '*suron ka pyaar aur andaz*,' the love and feel for each note. In this style, she learned many classic gharanas including Yaman, Shuddh Kalyan, Multani, and Puriya Dhanashri. In Poddarji's small apartment, he would conduct baithaks every Sunday in which he would perform and his students would rotate in giving *saath sangat*. 'We heard so many raags this way, and just by listening we learned so much.'

At college and in private tuitions, she also trained under Madhusudan Joshi, an Agra gharana vocalist who had trained under Ata Hussain Khan and Faiyaz Khan. Under him, it became clear that she was drawn to Agra gharana *gayaki*, with its playful exploration of rhythm and lyrics, as well as the abstract world of the *nom tom alap*.

She remembers him with fondness. 'Joshi master was such a thorough gentleman. He had no airs about him at all, and would always be found wearing a simple dhoti and kurta. He would come home two to three times a week, and when he came, not a second was wasted. I would lay out the chadar and take out the tanpura. He would immediately start the class – there was no talking to me or my father. He didn't have the habit of wasting time. I learned many of the special raags of Agra gharana from him: Khambavati, Nand, Barwa, Nat Kedar. *Alapi* (general *alap* phrases) were taught through *nom tom*, and he had a beautiful and delicate way of approaching the *sur* in *nom tom*, a way of gradually increasing the *laya* throughout the *alap*. Though I heard him use the approach often, he didn't make me do it too much. Perhaps at that time, the feeling was that female artists should not sing *nom tom alap*. I don't agree, I do it, but very few do.'

The musical culture in Baroda was rich and active, serving as a performance hub that featured many greats. 'I've heard Pandit Bhimsen Joshi at least ten times, and also Gangubai Hangal, Mallikarjun Mansur, Nivruttibua, Basavaraj Rajguru, Jasraj, Parveen Sultana. We listened to everyone without any ideas of gharana and learned so much.'

Soon enough, Shubhadaji's serious musical passion would lead her to new and unexpected experiences. After she completed her college degree, she went on a short holiday with a friend to Mumbai, where she stayed with her aunt in Dombivli. During this visit, her friend was very enthusiastic to introduce Shubhadaji to her cousin's small orchestral group. This ten-person ensemble consisted of two singers, tabla, accordion, harmonium, and octopad, and they were very eager to hear Shubhadaji. Shubhadaji was absolutely uninterested in listening to a mini orchestra set and refused to go. But with her friend's coaxing, she finally went along. She listened to them practise a bit, after which the group asked her to sing something. Reluctantly, she indulged them and sang a *natyageet*, for which she was accompanied by one of the band members, Satish, on harmonium. Though she did notice this tall and fair young man, nothing else about their interaction registered in her mind. Her friend, however, was intent on being a matchmaker. She asked Satish what he thought of this singer, and he told her how impressed he was by her singing and *tayyari*. That was enough to spark a fateful series of events in which Shubhadaji's family was informed about a nice, marriageable boy who expressed interest in this young lady and her music. Over the next few weeks, several meetings occurred between the two families. It was revealed that Satish's family members were serious music lovers, and many had completed the Sangeet Visharad diploma. Outside of music, they were a very educated lot – his four sisters included a Marathi professor, a Sanskrit professor, a doctor, and an engineer, not to mention Satish's MSc qualification in statistics. But, as is often the case with traditional alliances, when Satish's family met Shubhadaji, they had reservations about the height difference between her and their son. Soon after she sang a *bandish* in Maru Bihag and a *bhajan*, they forgot such trivialities. 'I was so thin and fragile, I was hardly at the age to get married, I was just twenty-one to twenty-two. But he liked my music. Finally, he told his family, forget about height and weight, I like her. After everyone heard me, they also liked me.'

Adjusting to a new family was certainly a transition

for Shubhadaji – she was particularly afraid of her elderly mother-in-law, who was a strict matriarchal figure in the house. However, the family's commitment to her *talim* and career provided the support many women require when balancing family life with the demands of a musical career. Shubhadaji's successes and joys were equally shared by Satish, who spearheaded her search for a guru, and became more involved in his own engagement with classical music, often travelling with her and accompanying her on harmonium for concerts.

After Gajananbua's passing, Shubhadaji again found herself in the position of seeking a guru, but this time, with a more specific intention: to deepen her engagement with the Agra *gayaki*, the style that she was most attracted to. During the annual Aundh Mahotsav organized in memory of Gajananbua's father, Anant Manohar Joshi, Bua had invited a younger Mumbai based Agra vocalist, Babanrao Haldankar, to perform. 'There were very few musicians whom Bua appreciated – Kane Bua, Limaye Bua, Gindeji, Kaikiniji, Madhusudan Kanetkarbua, and Babanraoji. Even while Bua was alive, he told me that there is much to absorb from Babanraoji, and that I should go to him to learn. He had the greatness and humility to tell me to go to another guru.'

At the time, Shubhadaji and family had moved to Badlapur, a suburb even farther removed from the city centre. Babanraoji lived in Opera House, sixty kilometres and a two-hour train ride away. Shubhadaji's schedule continued to be tight, though her children were older. After waking up early and sending them off to school, she would catch the 6.45 a.m. local train to Grant Road to reach Babanraoji's home by 9 a.m. If the trains were running late, she would be in a fix, either late to her class or late to return by the time her children were back from school. 'It was cut to cut timing. I used to go once or twice a week for *talim* like this.'

After the hustle of her morning travel, Shubhadaji would arrive in an atmosphere that was quite the opposite: a rather laid back and relaxed home setting. When she reached his house, Babanraoji would usually be heading in for a bath, starting his day at a leisurely pace. 'I used to think, arre, he hasn't even taken a bath yet? When will he come? When will we sit to sing? Forty-five minutes to an hour would pass like this. He was like that, a very different type of person.'

When it came to the music, Shubhadaji was clear that she wanted training in *gayaki* above all. In particular, she sought Babanraoji's specific brand of *laykari* (rhythm-driven improvisation), '*jhula jaise*' – a specific swinging and playful movement connecting phrases with moments of surprise accents. This rhythmic play required a delicacy: '*nazakat se, laad pyaar se*, that was his specialty.' Babanraoji's spontaneous rhythmic treatment of *dhamar*, a vibrant and rhythmically oriented form that Agra gharana musicians specialize in presenting, was also something that appealed to Shubhadaji. Though this approach to rhythm required years of effort around taal and *laya*, it was not calculated or mathematical. It was born out of what emerged on the spot, requiring a deep feel for taal *ka andaz*.

Shubhadaji emphasized that clear diction and connection to the *bhav* of the words of the *bandish* were important features of the Agra approach. 'I always say that *bhav* is important in everything we sing. It should not be dry singing. It might be in *sur*, but it is not effective. Even classical music is *bhav sangeet*. Even *laykari* has *bhav*, it must. Babanraoji taught me how to soften my big voice when required.'

With each raag that he taught her, Babanraoji brought Shubhadaji's attention to the treatment and approach to each note (*suron ke lagav*), and the importance or status of each note in the larger framework of the raag (*suron ke darje*). How is the *komal gandhar* in Bhimpalasi different from Darbari Kanada? He would demonstrate these differences through phraseology and *bandish*es. Unlike Gajananbua, he allowed her to take notes and record classes. Temperamentally very different from Bua, he was generous in his praise, and as Shubhadaji had begun composing herself, she often shared her own compositions for feedback. After appreciating them, he would ask her to record them and send them to him so he could learn them too.

Though *talim* took place once or twice a week over a period of ten years, Shubhadaji experienced a different style and pace of learning. Her foundations with

Gajananbua made new learning highly accelerated. She added rare and gharana specific raags to her repertoire: Lachari Todi, Khem Kalyan, Shree, Barwa, Anand Bhairav, Sarang, Duliya Sarang, Jog, and many *bandish*es of Ustad Khadim Hussain Khan (Babanraoji's guru).

She began merging her conceptual understanding with aesthetic features of Babanrao's *gayaki* to find her own voice. 'In Babanraoji's style he sings *nom tom*, and there is a specific way in which he approaches and utters the notes. I applied that in my own *alap*. Then as I move forward, I increase the *laya*, because the Gwalior style moves in a rather racy *madhyalaya*. Within that, sometimes I insert words and weave it into the *laya*, in the Gwalior style. Then I move forward to do more Agra oriented *laykari*. In this way, I find a confluence of the two so that it becomes one form. It helps that there are similarities between these two styles. If there is a raag that is specific to the Gwalior, I will only sing it in that style. And if it is sung in both, like Shree, I will balance both styles. I have explored this through my *riyaz*. I have developed my own *gayaki*.'

In the spirit of seeking and cultivating a distinct style, Shubhadaji also received training from Jaipur gharana stalwart, Padmavati Shaligram. She had grown up listening to Padmavatiji extensively on the radio, idolizing her music. It had always been a dream to study with her. Specifically, she wanted to learn Padmavatiji's style of *thumri*. The Paradkar family had moved back to the city centre, from Badlapur to Bandra, where her husband's job was based. She crossed paths with

Padmavatiji during the Aundh music festival (in memory of Gajananbua's father, Anant Manohar Joshi), in which Shubhadaji was involved organizationally. The festival had invited Padmavatiji to judge a competition. With great trepidation, Shubhadaji asked her if she could learn from her, expressing admiration for her rendition of *thumri*. Padmavatiji's personality was a stark contrast from Babanraoji's relatable and warm demeanour: she was strict and moody. 'Just as sweet as her music was, her own personality was *kadak* (harsh).'

Though Shubhadaji wanted to learn *thumri*, Padmavatiji insisted that she begin with raag and *khayal*. But when Shubhadaji began singing, Padamvatiji would angrily exclaim: 'Don't sing like Gajananrao and Babanrao!' She would reprimand her, but forgo her temper moments later when she would teach *thumri* towards the end of the class. While teaching her *khayal* in the Jaipur style, Shubhadaji remembers struggling to learn the famous complex Jaipur *taan* patterns. Like Gajananbua, Padamavatiji did not allow any writing or recording of the classes. One of her greatest takeaways while learning *thumri* was the importance and aesthetics of *ucchar*. In Padmavatiji's style of *thumri*, the lyrics took utmost importance – both in their meaning and as vehicles of sound emotion. *Ucchar* was not just a matter of pronunciation or diction – it was an aesthetic consideration, an exploration of the colours of vowels and their emotive shades. 'Arre! Marathi *ucchar nako karo*! (Hey! No Marathi pronunciation!)' she would scold.

She was referring to a diction that required the partial opening of sounds, much like a flower in various stages of bloom. While Marathi *ucchar* tends to be fully open and nakedly exposed, the *thumri ucchar*, like the play of the *thumri* itself, demands a partial revelation of sound that creates its own effect of coyness and enticing restraint of a lover.

She would make Shubhadaji explore all the major vowels – *akar*, *ukar*, *ekar*, *ikar*, *okar*. In the *thumri*, '*Aaj chale chaahe kaal*,' Padmavatiji would ask her: 'Which type of "aa" will you use here?' The shape of the *akar* was dependent upon the *bhav* of the *thumri* – she encouraged her to develop a more rounded *akar* sound. The pronunciation of 'l,' at the end of the word '*kaal*,' also required a mere grazing of the phonetic, audible in its impermanence. Through much repetition in class and *riyaz*, she made her incorporate these aspects of execution, as well as finer ornamental touches of *thumri*, like *khatka* and *murki*. This blend of aesthetic influences made an impact on Shubhadaji's approach to *khayal* as well.

In addition to *thumri* and *dadra*, Shubhadaji also trained in the form of *tappa* – a genre inspired by Punjabi folk music that features fast cascading patterns of notes, placed precisely within the words of the composition. She learned *tappa* during her frequent visits to Ujjain – her sister-in-law lived there – from a Gwalior gharana musician, Wagh master. '*Tappa* is a form that requires proper *talim* and lots of close listening,' she says. In addition to Wagh master, she was inspired by *tappa* renditions by Malini Rajurkar and Sharad Sathe.

Though Shubhadaji's multifaceted musical journey features training under an illustrious line of gurus, she is not a replica of any of them. She emerges as a singular voice, an amalgamation of thought, aesthetics, and *gayaki*. As a guru for almost forty-five years, she has crafted her own methodology of imparting the various aspects of her traditional *talim* to the modern-day student. She auditions her students and selects those who are at an advanced level and committed to music in a serious way, if not as a full-time profession. She balances a pace that keeps students engaged in a raag long enough, while also moving along and creating variety to keep them on their toes. Like she was taught, she also teaches a variety of *bandish*es in each raag. But what she appreciates most about the modern student is her inquisitiveness and the freedom with which she questions her gurus.

She encourages this openness of dialogue with her students. 'The current generation is very smart, they pick up fast. They have access to many recordings and they listen. And they also ask questions. I didn't have the courage to ask my gurus. They ask questions about the differences between raags, and I enjoy this, it makes me happy to have these discussions with them. As I teach, I show them the differences between similar raags and point out when it is an approach of Bua or Babanraoji. For instance, by showing Bilaskhani Todi and Komal Rishabh Asavari simultaneously, and how you would navigate these to keep them separate. What is the *lagav* of *rishabh* in each of these? By comparing these raags, it makes it easier for them to remember these details.'

And while she trains her students in her *gayaki*, she allows them to apply this knowledge as they may choose, even if that means different musical genres. Some students have established themselves as reputed classical vocalists: Manjusha Kulkarni Patil, Mugdha Vaishampayan, her daughter Rashmi Sule, Deepika Bhide Bhagwat, and Aishwarya Rao, to name a few. She also has students who have had successful careers in the film music industry, including Shalmali Kholgade and the Mahadevan sisters M.M. Manasi and M.M. Monissha.

Interestingly, the process of teaching further fuelled Shubhadaji's passion for composition, which she began exploring as early as her days as a Masters student at Baroda. There were times when she wasn't entirely convinced of the aesthetics of a traditional *bandish* – for instance, in the *vilambit khayal* '*Nike ghungariya*' in raag Bilaskhani Todi, the phonetic 'u' is placed on the *sam*. Vocally, she felt that this was an awkward vowel to highlight at every first beat, motivating her to compose her own *bandish* (*Itni araj mori*) in the same raag. As a guru, if she was not satisfied with a *bandish*, she would compose something that would be more suitable for her students.

Even if there is a specific impetus (to teach or to perform a new composition), the creative process has always been an organic and inspired one, not forced or contrived. When an idea or a moment happens to spark a musical thought, Shubhadaji captures that spirit and channels it into a *bandish*. She has composed in raags including Komal Rishabh Asavari, Bhoop, Nand, Vibhas, and many more. A *bandish* that holds deep personal value is one that was composed after the death of Gajananbua in raag Kaunsi Kanada: '*Man laagyo re tumhare charanan ko; Guru ke bin kacchu na suhaave*.' Her pen name, Shubharang, can be found in the poetry of her collection of eighty compositions. She has taught many of these *bandish*es to her students.

During the early stages of her career, Shubhadaji remembers nervously scanning newspapers for her concert reviews. It was a period when music critics were knowledgeable, balanced, and largely impartial in their assessment of performances. One of the critiques she faced was that her music was too 'masculine' and 'aggressive.' The masculinity in her music was specifically attributed to her active and lively engagement with *laykari* and taal.

'I reflected on this and reduced it a bit. I increased the time and emphasis on *sur* and *alap*. I worked on this and slightly changed my *gayaki*, because I felt there was some truth to the criticism. I felt that I may be doing too much *laykari*. But I still do *nom tom alap* because I like it. I don't think that is too masculine. But why do we need to bring gender into this? It is unfair. Understand an artiste as an artiste, not as a female or male.'

Her words resonated with my experience as a female student and practitioner of the Agra *gayaki*. Often, I have been told that my music is masculine, or that some elements of my rendition do not suit a female vocalist. I would wonder, what is the place for gender in the abstract space of music, a space that one would presume transcends social constructs? But the question persists.

How is gender performed in *khayal*, and what are the markers of gender-specific vocal practices? The idealized feminine voice in Hindustani music is often characterized by qualities such as tonic pitch (position of *sa*), vocal timbre, voice throw, dynamic range, phonetic diction, treatment of notes, and techniques of improvisation that privilege melodic over rhythmic engagement. The 'open throated' singing of the Agra gharana – which includes a robust, unmodulated voice throw, a thicker and dense sound over sustained periods of time, has been associated aesthetically and physiologically with masculinity. The ornamentation of notes – particularly heavy *gamak* or deep *meend*, have also become gendered. Women who present *nom tom alap*, as well as extensive *laykari*, are often scrutinized under a different lens than their male counterparts.

Shubhadaji's approach to the *nom tom alap* takes all these factors into consideration. The core of her aesthetic understanding of the *nom tom* lies in the phonetic nuances. The syllables used in a *nom tom* (*ri*, *re*, *ta*, *na*, *ne*, *num* for example) are believed to be derived from the phrase, *Hari Om Ananta Narayana*. These seemingly small phonetic building blocks are loaded with '*aas*,' a shape, arc and resonance that make them deeply emotive messengers of sound. The beauty of a plain *akar* is not something that

Shubhadaji disputes, but she finds greater possibilities in the exploration of a wide palette of phonetics. 'It is my special observation that in *oo-kar*, *ay-kar*, *ee-kar* and *uh-kar*, there is a different joy that is experienced.' It is not only the sounds, but the bridges between these sounds, the connective paths – a phonetic *meend* of sorts – that blends the infinite shades between vowels while traversing a musical gradient. The seeds for this approach were planted in her mind by her early training with Joshi master in Baroda.

She acknowledges that some early masters of the gharana exaggerated the phonetic palette and voice throw, creating a kind of melodrama that was not well received by listeners. Shubhadaji emphasizes the importance of individual understanding of the voice – each singer must have an awareness of the qualities of her voice, and how to achieve an uncompromised version of the desired sound within those parameters.

She has explored this within her own voice to achieve the results she desires. '*Phaink* is throwing the voice. I have a big voice, so I sing very openly. But within that, modulation of the voice is very important. You shouldn't sing in one tone throughout. This is difficult, that is why very few people sing *nom tom*. And it is a task that requires strength – it is not superficial singing from the upper throat. It requires abdominal singing. People call this type of treatment (*she demonstrates a jerky gamak movement*) *purush ka gana*, manly singing. But how did female artists also sing like this? Maybe not as forcefully as men, but by applying a little weight, why can't they do it? I certainly do.

'*Shobha nahi deta* lady artists *ko aise gana.* It doesn't suit lady artists to sing like this. But I say, if you keep balance in mind as you sing, then it sounds very nice. You have to think according to your tonal quality. Whatever song I sing, my main criteria is that there should be sweetness. This is the angle from which we can also do *nom tom*, with the appropriate modulations. With delicacy, softness, and weight also. The difficult question is, if you want softness, then how can you also apply weight? It seems like a contradiction, but it is possible, though it is difficult. Keeping weight in the voice while maintaining a sweet tone. It is in the technique,' she reflects.

Some of Shubhadaji's students have relatively thinner voices – in this case, she asks them to fortify their sound. 'If you always sing so sweetly, how will that work? If your meal only consists of gulab jamun and nothing else – no roti, rice, or bhaji – can anyone eat like that? How much sugary singing will you do? Even in music, you need all flavours. I always tell this to my students.'

The decision to present a *nom tom alap* in a concert, and in which raag to do so, depends upon various factors. According to Shubhadaji, some raags lend themselves well to deep exploration: Miyan Malhar, Darbari, Shree, to name a few. The second factor is the audience for whom she is singing: are they seasoned listeners or relatively new to the experience? Perhaps the abstract nature of *nom tom alap* demands more from the listener, in terms of experience and familiarity with the form.

—

Although I didn't recognize it at first, it became apparent to me with time that Shubhadaji's approach to her gayaki and teaching possesses feminist undertones. This is evident in her ideas about voice and gender in the Agra gayaki, and also in the more practical stances she takes to encourage her female students. She empathizes and supports women as they navigate a tough career amidst various cultural expectations. She is honest about the realities she has observed for many Indian women, and the challenges that plague a musician. 'After singing, we have to get up and do all the housework. My girls come here and take class until evening, around 7 p.m. Then they go home to cook for their family. For any female artist, vocal or instrumental, I have extra love. Because I know they have many responsibilities, and it is very difficult to manage a house, family and your music. At home you have to manage your children, their studies. Usually, it is only the woman who does this, both do not. The complaint is that I encourage female artists too much. For men who are artists, what do they have to do? They don't have to do anything at home. If guests come, I will make tea and take care of them. If somebody is there to help me, that is a different thing.'

These comments reminded me of many conversations I

have with friends about work-life balance and distribution of labour within a household. The conversation is a reality in any professional sphere. But, as a female musician who works from home, a space in Indian culture which is largely seen as the woman's domain, professional musicians cannot easily find the boundaries between their everyday life and their musical 'work.'

Despite the variety of challenges that have come up in the course of her life, the encouraging atmosphere nurtured by her family was critical in her musical career. She thinks of the many students who have come to her and given up music after marriage – 'If that *mahaul* is not there, it is very difficult to sustain.' She reflects fondly on the support she received from her family – with tears in her eyes, she points to a photo of her husband, Satish, who passed away a few years back. Her daughter, Rashmi, continues in the field of classical music, and though her son Ranjeet is a music lover, he has not pursued music professionally.

Through her career, she has travelled all over India, the US, and Bangkok as a performer and guru. Though the modern performance scenario has changed, requiring musicians to publicize and advocate for themselves through various modalities, she doesn't subscribe to this way of operating. 'I have never done this. At this age, why will I start? There is no need. Those who know me know me. I tell my students, sing well. Keep your principles in mind as you manage professionally. Don't go begging for programmes. Opportunities will come to music that is true and genuine. I believe it. And is it necessary to have four programmes in a month?'

Shubhadaji is optimistic about the women who are the future of Hindustani music. 'This generation is filled with so many smart and talented young women. The future is honestly very bright.' Despite the waves of disillusionment I have felt in the professional sphere of music, conversations with Shubhadaji leave me hopeful and inspired. She has walked the walk of womanhood and musicianship, creativity and personal innovation, quietly shifting gender norms and barriers through her music and way of being.

3

SUDHINDRA BHAUMIK

The Call of Music: Part I

'MY FATHER NEVER EVEN TOUCHED ME.'

It is rare, but occasionally a child comes into the world with a deep knowing – filled with answers, rather than questions, about a life that has barely begun. It is a preternatural clarity of sorts, in which the child possesses an unusual wisdom and fearlessness to face the world at any cost to fulfil their calling. Sometimes it seems as though an adult is inhabiting the body of a child, robbed of an innocence that precedes the burdens of adulthood. Yet, this type of child feels no regret, remaining fiercely committed to this deep-rooted intuition that is an unstoppable force of its own.

Jogendranath Bhaumik was one of the precocious chosen ones. Born into a family of farmers in the early 1900s in what would become East Pakistan (and later Bangladesh), he knew early on that farming was not his path. While his family struggled to make ends meet, he dreamed of receiving a formal education. It was his golden ticket to a new life of opportunity and upward financial mobility. He didn't wait long to follow his heart. At the age of eight, he had the presence of mind and grit to leave his family and village in search of a school, any school at all. In early twentieth century British India, schools were few and far between in rural areas such as his town of Maheshkhola.

Thus began his odyssey, the quest for a basic education. As a young child without money, shelter or food, at times he begged, at times he borrowed, and at times he was employed as household help, all while studying in a local school where he had managed to wrangle admission. The mythic legend of his struggle supersedes the details – but the proof is in the pudding. Jogendranath completed his education until the level of IA – Intermediate Arts – an academic diploma equivalent to a high school degree under the colonial education system. He had in fact partially completed his BA as well, but a job opportunity in the district of Jessore pulled him straight into the working world and his aspiration for a professional life would become a reality.

Jessore, situated in present-day Bangladesh, was a prominent city centre and the administrative capital for many villages in the district. Jogendranath was a clerk in the District Board Office, a position that allowed him greater social capital and baseline economic stability. In this momentum of good fortune, marriage was also part and parcel. Jogendranath and his young wife Bindubasini nurtured a home that hosted many visitors from all parts –

farmers and villagers who came to Jessore to settle land or legal disputes knew they could spend a night or more at the Bhaumik household while sorting out their problems. Even if they arrived at odd hours of the night, Jogendranath never turned anyone in need of help away, often waking up to make them a meal or a cup of tea.

The Bhaumik family expanded, and over a period of roughly eleven years, they went from two to nine. After giving birth to three boys and three girls, Bindubasini lost her seventh child shortly after he was born. Despite the anguish of the loss, the couple conceived again and added one more son to the clan. The eighth child was born healthy, completing a long line of children. Jogendranath saw the parallels to another significant son born in the eighth position – Krishna. His name must be Kaala, he declared definitively, invoking one of the many affectionate names for Krishna. He had no doubt that his child, like Krishna, would not only survive but thrive in the face of whatever life threw at him. He had the grace and protection of his namesake, after all.

Many close calls in Kaala's life certainly proved time and again that this was the case. At age three, while standing next to a lamp during Durga puja, his brand-new oversized kurta caught fire and spread rapidly to his entire body. Enveloped in flames, he developed nearly fatal third-degree burns. But with natural remedies and rest, the resilient child recovered and soldiered on.

Six months later, Kaala and his friend were playfully taken by the hanging fruit of a jackfruit tree. His friend devised a plan, only plausible in the mind of a child: he would climb the tree and cut the fruit with his wooden cutter while Kaala would wait below and catch it. Kaala's accident-prone streak continued – the cutter slipped out of his friend's hand, the wooden handle hitting Kaala's head and then bouncing on to his chest. He was left with a one-inch-deep wound on his chest. But again, the mysterious forces surrounding Kaala prevailed and he healed.

Much later, in his twenties, Kaala tried to board a moving tram but was thrown off in the process. As he lay injured in the middle of a busy main road, a double decker bus steadily approached from behind. But luck would have it that it had to make a stop just a few metres before it would have hit him. Kaala survived again.

Kaala needed the invisible hand of his protector, and perhaps Jogendranath was guided by this premonition when he declared the nickname for his last born. Five months after Kaala's birth, Jogendranath died in his late forties from bone tuberculosis of the spine. The family speculates that he contracted the highly contagious disease from his British supervisor at the District Board Office, whose home he visited often for urgent administrative matters. He was already severely ill by the time Kaala was born.

'My father never even touched me,' Kaala remembers.

And thus, Jogendranath's compelling journey was tragically and abruptly ended while Kaala's was barely beginning.

Like most days in Mumbai, the sultry weather drapes around the city like a velvet coat of humidity. I am on autopilot – get off at Mumbai Central station and cross several busy intersections, weaving through traffic and the curses of drivers, passing clusters of stationery and sari shops. The fuchsia bougainvillea outside the Parsi fire temple is my beacon that the destination is near – Talmakiwadi Co-operative Housing Society. Signs inside the society proudly proclaim that it is Asia's oldest housing co-operative, established in 1941 by the Kanara Saraswat community. The further inside you get, the more distant the chaos and rumblings of the city becomes.

I am dripping with sweat and have not even completed the most strenuous part of this short and otherwise undemanding walk – the four flights of stairs I have to climb before reaching my guru's residence. When I ring the doorbell, I am breathing heavily and my kurta is practically fused into my skin with sweat. He opens the door, a tall and towering figure with piercing eyes hidden beneath furrowing eyebrows, overshadowed by his long, white and typically sage-like beard. He nods his head to acknowledge my presence and I enter.

To call this space where he lives a 'residence,' as I just did, is misleading, to say the least. It is a room, approximately 120 square feet in size. As you enter, you get a view of his entire living space in one glance: a mattress on the floor, computer and desk, a steel cupboard and bookshelf, and behind a curtain that is usually open, there is a kitchen space and bathroom. Students sit on the same mattress for class while he sits on the computer chair, instructing from above. A photograph from his younger days hangs on the wall behind him, a meta moment for the student who can see both present day and erstwhile guruji at the same time during a lesson.

He has lived alone in this single room for the last thirty years. In this space, he teaches students from morning to night, does his own *riyaz* and *chintan* (reflection), reading and self-learning, cooking and cleaning, yoga and meditation. Every time I enter, as I wait for my panting to subside and breath to resume its normal pace, I am reminded of the triviality of my complaints about Mumbai life. The space holds an energy of deep *sadhana* – it seems to be telling me: minimal living, maximum focus.

'*Kya karna hai aaj*?' he asks in his typical manner, urgent and direct. Let's get down to business, and business means only one thing: music. His speech matches his lifestyle: an economy of words. No chit chat, no formalities or niceties, no social lubrication.

I fumble in my response, making some long-winded answer to a simple question until I finally get to the crux, the current raag of choice.

The Radel electronic tanpura is already playing; it plays continuously in his room. I hear it in the background whenever I call him, whether it is 10 a.m. or 10 p.m. Because he teaches over forty students, all one-on-one, he spends the day singing in many different pitches and voice ranges. Most singers would experience vocal fatigue and injury from this kind of pitch fluctuation, but his voice is resonant and malleable, traversing octaves while teaching females and males.

I request raag Puriya. Sometimes we would work on a raag for a few weeks, at times it would be completely new, sometimes we'd revisit something I had learned before to get a fresh perspective that only time and distance can bring. None of this matters. On cue, like a jukebox, he immediately launches into a *nom tom alap*, a trademark style of free improvisation in the Agra gharana. I can hardly detect a moment for gathering his thoughts or shifting from the raag he was teaching in the previous lesson. The first phrase he utters lands into the personality of the raag like a dart in a bull's eye. This happens only when the stars of the musical axis align: precise knowledge and execution of phraseology, a voice that can follow the mind on command, and a heart that leads the entire process and keeps the raag connected to its emotional source.

His music is *bhav*-laden and his voice is built with *pukaar*. *Pukaar* – that elusive quality of vocal expression that creates a magnetic pull with the listener, inducing a moment of goosebumps or a flutter in the heart. It is not necessarily about *what* is sung, but *how* it is sung. When the quality and texture of the voice alone embodies the emotion in its full manifestation. The notes and phrases become secondary. Literally, the calling, it is an appeal from the voice to the outer world.

Pathos of loss, pain and hopefulness shine through his Puriya. At least that is how it resonates with me, but for him perhaps it is just another language in which he can converse. Each raag is its own language and he is a multilinguist. I feel like I'm standing under Niagara Falls, trying to collect water with an eye dropper. I am missing so much but whatever I collect is precious.

Time stops for me during the lesson. I have to be able to replicate anything he sings; I have to understand the structure of the raag; I have to understand the *bhav* of the music; I have to imbibe the nuances, but ultimately, I have to *sing*, not think.

'What do you want to say? You have to say something and mean it, no beating around the bush,' he says, not about my speaking but my singing. Both seem to be applicable.

The doorbell rings, the next student has arrived. My head is swimming with the ideas I have heard, trying to hold on to them tightly and also grasp the bigger picture before it escapes like vapour. I go to touch his feet before leaving and notice his fingers – I see patches of black marks still present from the childhood burns he survived.

—

At thirty-six, Bindubasini was a mother of seven and a widow. She did not have time to grieve or even complain of her misfortune. Survival was priority.

The family had to leave Jessore. Without Jogendranath's income, they couldn't sustain themselves there any longer. They soon moved to Hidiya, a largely farming-centred village in Phultala district. Bindubasini's brother, who owned and managed farmland in Hidiya, invited her to come and stay with his family as they navigated this new transition. The eight of them moved there and began a new life for the next few years, the children mostly passing their time playing football and fishing while only the eldest son, Shourendranath, continued his studies and began his college education with the support of his uncle. When her brother offered to train her children to be farmers to work on his land, Bindubasini refused. She was resolute that her children would be educated, following the footsteps of their father. She was not allured by the security or comfort that her brother's proposition offered, no matter how dire her situation may have been. She would see to it that the Bhaumik children would follow the academic path at all costs.

As Shourendranath, or Bar da, as the children called him, excelled in his studies, he also saw that his siblings were idling their time away. Concern about their future took root, so much so that when he was offered a job in the radar section of the Air Force, he decided to take the job even though it meant that he wouldn't complete his degree. When he received his first paycheck, the first thing he did was finance his family's move to West Bengal, where they had the promise of better schooling for all of his siblings.

Moving from Hidiya to West Bengal in 1949 was a messy affair – crossing borders from what was East Pakistan at that time to India post the relatively newly defined Partition required many formalities and security checks. Nothing was too daunting for Bindubasini. When they finally crossed there were ten of them. Bindubasini's eldest daughter, Parulbala, was already married and settled with her new family in East Bengal. That left her with her remaining six children and three of her brother's children whom she chose to take under her wing. Her brother had lost his wife in the recent past and remarried – in that transition, his children were not getting the attention they required. In a gesture of support to him, she took them along as the whole lot embarked on the next phase.

They made it safely to Simul Tala, another farming village a few kilometres outside the city of Krishnanagar where Bindubasini's sister, Sudhamukhi, lived. Bar da made it a point to enrol all of his siblings in schools in the area so no further time was lost. Kaala was enrolled in the first standard at the village school where Sudhamukhi, or Maasi ma as they called her, was the headmistress. The other siblings were enrolled in different schools, but all would walk two to three kilometres every day to reach the school, come back home in the evening and play football for some time before they got back to their studies and finally went to sleep. The routine continued for several years, and the Bhaumik home was so known in the area for its studious atmosphere that children from nearby villages used to carry their kerosene lanterns and come to the house just to have a place for focused study, heading back home after they had finished.

With the financial and moral support of her eldest son, Bindubasini managed to look after her family to the best of her abilities. Sudhamukhi procured a small piece of land for the family to live and farm on – they grew basic staples that were easy to cultivate at low cost: chillies, tomatoes, cauliflower, eggplant. Buying vegetables from the market was often unaffordable, and the family would manage with whatever was grown. Some days when ingredients were scarce, she would make a paste of onion and garlic and mix it with rice for the family. 'For us, it was like amrut (nectar),' Kaala recalls.

'She was a lioness,' he says about his mother. Tough as nails, strict and resourceful. She would go to the market and barter – buying paddy, converting it to rice, and then selling it back to earn some extra money. She was most famous for her skills as a midwife – it is not known when or how she acquired the ability, but she was the first person to be called when women of the village and neighbouring areas went into labour. Her commanding and unshakeable presence, along with her reputation of being the mother of a family of studious and cerebral children, earned her a special place of respect in her community.

Despite the economic hardships that persisted in day-to-day life, the Bhaumiks were enriched by a cultural atmosphere largely nurtured by their local community. Every evening before dinner, they would gather for music, talks, drama, dance, or prayers. In the midst of these activities, Kaala picked up folk songs, Rabindra Sangeet (songs composed by Tagore), *kirtan*, modern film songs heard on the radio, and even the tabla.

Day and night passed in this manner, and one day a pensive Kaala asked his cousin, 'What is it that we are supposed to do in this lifetime? Why are we here?' To which she replied, 'You are not supposed to ask this question. Whatever your elders tell you to do, you do. That is your job.'

He remained quiet, but was not satisfied with the answer. 'There was something in me that yearned for something larger, but I didn't know what that was.' At the time, there was only one goal to speak of: survival. Dreaming and philosophizing about life and the future were luxuries.

Eventually, time and the fortuity of circumstance would take Kaala closer to the answers he so deeply sought. Meanwhile, life was moving ahead for the Bhaumiks. As all the children excelled in their education, the time came for them to move yet again, this time closer to Kolkata, so they could have the choice of the many engineering colleges in the big city. There were no engineering colleges in Krishnanagar at the time.

They moved to the suburb of Sonarpur, but despite being in a big city, they were still without electricity and studying by the light of kerosene lamps as they did in Simul Tala and Hidiya. Kaala entered standard nine at a school in the upmarket Ballygunge neighbourhood. Particularly because of his high math scores, he was admitted to the well-reputed Jagadbandhu Institution two years later –

like his siblings, he too was following all the prescribed steps to success.

'We were told, academics is the only thing we have: do well in studies, otherwise we are doomed.' And they did more than well. The Bhaumik children shined in mathematics and engineering, and Kaala never questioned that he would attend Jadavpur Engineering College, like his brothers and sister, both rank-holding alumni. But after he aced his Higher Secondary exam, it was one of his friends who asked him casually if he had applied to IIT, the prestigious Indian Institute of Technology Universities across the country. Kaala innocently replied, 'No, I already have a seat in Jadavpur Engineering College.' Astounded, the friend told him not to miss out on the opportunity and urged him to at least apply and see what happens.

Without any preparation at all, Kaala took his entrance exam and was called back for an interview at Kharagpur. On his way there, his wallet was pickpocketed – which not only contained money and essentials but also his registration card for Jadavpur Engineering College. Perhaps this sealed his fate even before the interview was complete, because shortly after, he was admitted to IIT Kharagpur as a student of metallurgy.

While many families would celebrate and dote upon a child accepted into any of the IITs, things were business as usual for the Bhaumiks. It was yet another event in a sequence of events that comprised life, noteworthy if at all only as another task to be completed, and practical arrangements were made and nothing else made of the matter.

Transition from village life to a cosmopolitan university campus was challenging for Kaala. Despite being in a vibrant college town with young students from all over the country, he felt quite alone. He was on a very tight budget – a small scholarship supplemented by money sent by Bar da was just enough to manage month to month, but there was no extra cushion that would allow an occasional movie or chaat. In fact, Kaala had taken a vow before starting his education at IIT that he would not watch a single movie for the next five years.

While friends and entertainment may not have distracted him from his studies, there seemed to be invisible strings that kept pulling Kaala towards his musical inclinations. Before he had even dug his heels into his new surroundings, he was a target for the notorious 'raggers' of the IIT culture. Cornered by a group of bullies and forced to climb to the top of a loft area meant for luggage storage, Kaala found himself crouched over, looking down at his bullies not knowing what was next. To his surprise, and perhaps theirs as well, when they asked him to sing, he was at ease singing anything from Hemant Kumar tunes to Tagore. When he ran out of songs he could sing from memory, the raggers asked him to repeat the same tunes over and over until they had their fill. Finally, they not only allowed him to climb back down, but offered complete protection on campus whenever he needed it. Their leader proclaimed, 'You are a singer. Your ragging ends here. If anybody tries to rag you, you mention my name.'

Following his instincts, Kaala immersed himself in the cultural activities of his hall, participating in music competitions and festivals by singing, playing tabla and even guitar. Through these gatherings, he became friends with another student, Ranjit Kumar, who sang semi-classical repertoire like *thumris* and *dadras*. Until now, Kaala had only been interested in popular and folk music – in fact he decidedly disliked classical music and could not relate to or understand what classical musicians were doing when they sang. But after Ranjit opened up his eyes to this new genre, Kaala's aversion to classical music softened and many questions arose about this new form and how it worked. But where could he find the answers? Ranjit told him about his guru, Mr Shukla, who taught music in a school in Bihar. Kaala was intrigued, but that didn't help him as long as he was in Kharagpur. Also, he couldn't afford to take any lessons in music, nor were there any Hindustani classical music teachers in Kharagpur. He would have to continue with self-learning for now until opportunities presented themselves to him.

He was so engrossed in his musical extracurricular activities that his grades started slipping. It was a wake-up call that his priorities had shifted, so he took drastic measures to rectify this – he punctured and ripped the soft leather top of his tabla in half so that he could no longer play! Just looking at it served as a visceral reminder of the distance he needed to keep from music to stay on the academic path.

As a result of this, Kaala missed the cut off for First Class by less than one percent. But life moved on, he graduated and returned home to Sonarpur in search of a job in the field of metallurgy. The year was 1968 and the country was going through a recession – new graduates struggled to get jobs, and for the first time in many years, Kaala was anchorless. His mind kept drifting back to Mr Shukla in Bihar – if only he could meet him and start the music lessons he had been seeking.

Parables abound about the struggle for the search for the perfect guru. *The guru will find you, don't seek him! The guru will appear to you at the right time and place in your life! Matches of guru and shishya are pre-determined karmic associations.* Perhaps clichés, perhaps profound truths. For Kaala, only one thing was true – for several decades, his gurus did not appear in his life with any ease or serendipity. And even after he found them, life circumstances didn't always allow his pursuit to flow with a quality of inexplicable mystical smoothness. But when something inside of him was awakened, it was as though a low burning flame suddenly received an extra gust of oxygen and for the first time he saw the potency of its luminosity. It couldn't be ignored any longer.

Kaala was back home with his family after graduating

from IIT. One morning, he left without telling anyone that he was leaving or where he was going. Possessed by a madness to find answers, he boarded a train to the hill station, Netarhat, Bihar. Over the next two days of his journey, he contemplated meeting the man who had been on his mind, Mr Shukla. Would he accept him as a disciple? Would he be the man with the answers?

Kaala managed to find the elusive guru at the famous Netarhat Residential school. He arrived at his doorstep unannounced – a stranger seeking a mentor. He introduced himself and went straight to the point.

'I am Sudhindra Bhaumik, I have come to ask if you will be my guru.'

Shuklaji was taken aback by his story. First, he expressed his concern that Kaala's family would be distraught over his sudden absence. Then he dropped the heavy news to this young twenty-something year old: 'I am not your guru, but you will find your guru in time, do not worry.'

Resigned to his fate with Shuklaji, Kaala made his way back home. He had to face the temporary ire of his family, but they understood that he was going through a phase of self-exploration and inner churning. As he tried to make sense of what his next steps would be, a friend told him about the Indian Institute of Management, another prestigious institution which could open up doors on the career path. Much like the way he applied to IIT, Kaala showed up for the IIM entrance exam with no preparation and aced it. He was admitted and began his degree in Operations Research and Production. Academics would continue to reign over the direction of his life.

The silver lining of this new journey was that he would be living in Kolkata, where music teachers were aplenty. After settling into the hostel, he went to meet the vocalist Pandit A.T. Kanan, a reputed and popular musician influenced by the style of Ustad Amir Khan. Kanan Saheb met Kaala and advised him to learn from his disciple, Pandit Vishwanath Sur. At the age of twenty-four, Kaala finally began his first formal lessons in music. Sur Saheb exposed him to various forms of *khayal*, several raags, and gave him a flavour of the canvas of Hindustani music. At long last, his journey in music was off to a start.

There were developments in other areas of his life; it wasn't all music and studies for Kaala in his mid-twenties. The Bhaumik family had expanded further – his siblings had married, and when Kaala was at home, he was with his mother, Bar da and Bar da's wife, Sulekha, or Bau di. Bar da and Kaala had a connection that went beyond that of merely being siblings. Perhaps it was the circumstances of Kaala's birth, their fourteen-year age difference, and the multiple roles that Bar da would inhabit for the youngest child of the family. One thing was clear – as much as possible, he always wanted to keep Kaala close to him.

Much like the big age gap and parental connection between Kaala and Bar da, Bau di and her younger sister Sucheta were ten years apart and virtually inseparable. Sucheta was always at the Bhaumik household after her sister got married, and Kaala and Sucheta developed a young friendship over many years of their adolescence. The two shared common interests like yoga, music and dance (she was trained in Rabindrik dance). They stayed in touch even while each of them went off to college, meeting again when they were back in Kolkata. The two had a natural and easy bond.

One day, while challenging each other to do various yoga poses, Sucheta raised the stakes without knowing how serious things were going to get. 'If you can do *Ustrasana* (bending backwards to touch the toes), then I will accept anything that you make me do.' Kaala thought about it for a split second and replied, 'Okay, if I do it, you must marry me!' He flexed easily into the asana and Sucheta, embarrassed and caught off guard, fled away in shyness.

The family had been observing the sparks between their two youngest members and decided to get them married while Kaala was studying at IIM. By his second year, their first son, Dhrubajyoti, was born, and Sucheta, Bar da, and Bau di, all lived together on Broad Street in Kolkata. Kaala would come home on the weekends to be with family while he was finishing his master's degree. Though his family life had begun, the course of his life was still largely unwritten.

All of his years of diligent studying finally paid off – after graduating from IIM, Kaala had a job offer from Kamani Metals and Alloys in Mumbai. Despite his academic achievements and coveted career path, the first question that came to his mind was always, 'How will I continue my music training?' His good friend from IIM, Ravi Koppikar, a sitar player himself, assured him that he was going to the best place. Koppikar told him about his brother-in-law, K.G. Ginde, who was a highly knowledgeable scholar and distinguished vocalist of the Agra gharana. He assured him that if he met him after settling down, he would put him on the right musical path.

After Kaala and his family moved to Mumbai, fortune would have it that Bar da was also transferred to Mumbai through his job with IBM. The families continued to live together, the brother-sister couples and their children, still together in a new city. They lived in Venus Apartments in Worli and the cosmopolitan world of Mumbai became home.

Soon after moving, Kaala met Gindeji and was directed to start his training with Pandit S.C.R. Bhat, Gindeji's senior guru bhai and vice principal of Vallabh Sangeetalay in Sion, Mumbai. Bhat Saheb, who was a disciple of scholar musician Pandit S.N. Ratanjankar for over thirty-five years, was patient and meticulous in expecting every phrase and composition to be replicated without even the slightest deviation. He would not lose his temper, but he would also not move on until he was satisfied that the student had sung to his standards. Kaala threw himself into his training in all the spare time he had.

While evenings and nights were spent learning raags and *khayal*s, the rest of the day was spent at a new job supervising the factory floor of Foisha Industrial Company, a manufacturer of tin cans. Straight from work at the factory in Thane, Kaala took the local train to Sion, reaching in time to catch the tail end of Bhat Saheb's last group class of the day, after which he would receive *seena-ba-seena* (face-to-face) training. He would get home at almost 11 p.m., and leave for work again in the morning by 6 a.m. This was his unbending routine, six days a week. There was literally not a minute to spare in his schedule, but somehow his music was soaring. This was the first time Kaala experienced a very focused and structured system of learning music: the nuances of many raags, a variety of compositions – *khayal*, *dhrupad* and *dhamar* – and the aesthetics of performance in Hindustani classical music. How do you unfold a raag? What are the pillars of improvisation, and how do you take flight from these posts? How does one make a conversation through notes?

It was hard for others to really comprehend what he was going through as something beyond a passion or hobby. When he received a promising job offer from Engineering Projects India Ltd in Delhi, he secretly wrote them a letter declining it. But when Bar da learned of this, he was so upset with Kaala that he didn't speak to him for the next few months. Things eventually returned to normal, but after a few years of togetherness, IBM transferred Bar da to Bengaluru and for the first time, the two brothers and sisters would be separated. Because they were no longer sharing living costs, staying in Worli became unfeasible. Kaala, Sucheta and Dhrubajyoti had to move to a lower-cost Worker's Colony in Chunabhatti, Sion. Living conditions were tough, and though they were able to find an English medium school for Dhrubajyoti, the struggles of daily living, commuting, and basic survival in a city like Mumbai were weighing heavily on everyone. Soon, Sucheta became pregnant with their second child. Bar da dropped in for a visit and saw the challenges they were facing – he insisted that mother and child come back to Bengaluru and stay with him.

Kaala would stay back alone in Mumbai and live without his family, adding a new set of obstacles each day for his survival. He moved to the suburb of Mulund to be closer to work, but between his travel from Thane to Sion for his classes, and then back home to Mulund, he was left with barely enough time for basic self-care. Kaala ate anything he could squeeze in during his commutes and he couldn't look after his health or nourishment for sheer lack of time between work, music, and the tough reality of long Mumbai commutes. But *talim* with Bhat Saheb was so engrossing and intoxicating that the musical high kept Kaala going despite all odds.

In his first fully classical public performance in Mumbai, one could say Kaala went rogue. The concert was held at his guru's institute, Vallabh Sangeetalaya, and he and his senior guru-bhai, Indudhar Nirody, were to perform a duet. Bhaumik and Nirody, as they were called by their musical community, had been preparing for the performance together, guided by Bhat Saheb in the nuances of duet performances. The concert day arrived, and like many at this venue, the audience was filled with learned musicians. The raag for the evening was Puriya Dhanashri, and after sitting on stage, something inexplicable happened to

Bhaumik. He became so possessed by Puriya Dhanashri and the energy of a live audience that poor Nirody could barely get a note in! But this was not held against him, as everyone seemed to understand that today was Bhaumik's moment – the music he had craved for almost three decades was finally bursting out of his body and soul. Musicians in attendance expressed hard won praise for his debut, but the biggest compliment were the tears that quietly escaped Bhat Saheb's eyes as he watched his shishya as a performer. Could it be that from Simul Tala to Mumbai, in his quest to find a guru and be seriously drenched in music, he had *finally* experienced the proper alignment of his stars? His calling, the *pukaar* of his life?

On his next visit to Mumbai, Bar da told Kaala that it was time to come back to Bengaluru and start a business together selling data punching card machines. The Mumbai experiment had to end – life apart was simply too hard now that their second son, Subroto, was also a new addition to the family. Kaala couldn't bear to disappoint his elder brother again, so he acquiesced, quit his job, put his music dreams on hold again, and made his way to another new city, Bengaluru.

4

SUDHINDRA BHAUMIK

The Call of Music: Part II

WINTER IN MUMBAI IS A SHORT-LIVED PHENOMENON that Mumbaikars spend the whole year either awaiting or reminiscing about. The weather is finally perfect – the light has a cinematic way of illuminating its gothic buildings, the amalgam of smells that accumulate in all the months of humidity seem to dissipate, and that ever so mild coolness in the ocean breeze suddenly makes life such a doable affair.

But for musicians, winter means concert season. Weekends and weekdays are filled with *mehfil*s or big stage events, artistes wait for their turn to shine after having spent the year hustling to get presenters to feature them in prime slots. Youngsters vie for coveted Youth Festival opportunities, and many trek across the city by bus, train, or cabs, to hear their contemporaries or aging stalwarts who don't grace the stage too often. Sometimes these concerts are glamorous and Page 3-esque, with celebrity sightings and diaphanous bejewelled saris flowing. They are held at air-conditioned venues, where somehow the lower the temperature, the more elite the gathering. Ladies break out their pashmina shawls as their teeth chatter in a *jugalbandi* with the tabla. Afterwards, drivers pick up industrial patrons in Mercedes-Benzes and Audis, and on the way home they lament about the decline in quality of classical music these days, but of course they will keep supporting it with their foundations and CSR initiatives, because, '*We must support our culture, na*?'

In an alternate universe, concerts fill suburban community halls, lined with plastic chairs that make flatulent noises with the smallest movement, the obligatory vinyl banner hanging crookedly behind a small stage. Clouds of dust emerge from dharris as the artiste sits down, and music is projected through an Ahuja sound system from the 1980s. 'Green rooms' – where the artistes tune their instruments and get into a meditative space before getting on stage – stink of the most concentrated urine imaginable from the attached loo that has not been cleaned for ages. Long introductory speeches are made where unedited bios are read verbatim. A chief guest is honoured and hyperbole oozes out of every honorific used. Every person remotely involved in the event is thanked and garlanded, and somewhere after this ocean of bhashan, the music finally starts. And despite all of these conditions, or maybe because of them, some of the most honest and exciting music happens here. Audiences are inches away from the performer and break out uncontrollably into '*kya baat hai*' or '*wah wah*' so often that the artiste eventually levitates with bliss. These suburban audiences don't just give away their *daad*, or praise, unless it is well deserved. They know the dos and don'ts of the raags, they know when the artiste has missed the *sam*, and when you say you are the 'torchbearer' of a gharana, they actually know what that entails and expect to see it in the music – in the choice of compositions, in *alap* development, in *taan* patterns, in *laykari*. If not, they will come up to you after the concert and give it to you straight.

On a Sunday morning in late February, I relished that the Mumbai winter was lingering well past its typical timeline, and I ventured to Vashi, Navi Mumbai. Bhaumikji was performing at the Gandharva Maha Vidyalaya, a concert in memory of Pandit Dinkar Kaikini, one of his gurus. He hadn't told me if I would be accompanying him on tanpura, but I had to be prepared for any eventuality. I reached in time to hear the young artiste before him, but halfway into his recital a few of us students were whisked away to a green room to be with him as he tuned and warmed up with the accompanists.

He was ruminating over singing Desi, a rather esoteric raag that is rare to hear in current times. Sung close to noon, just as the crisp energy of morning starts morphing into a languorousness that solidifies post-lunch, Desi has undulating microtones that seem to pull the listener into the guilty pleasures of a leisurely afternoon in an arid climate where time stops. Sometimes it reminds of its neighbouring sister-raag Jaunpuri, other times of the iconic raag of the Agra gharana, Barwa. This delicate dance around these common areas is known as the balance between *avirbhav* and *tirobhav*. *Avirbhav*, being the unequivocal and staid path of the raag, versus *tirobhav*, the intentional and skilful entry into overlapping sonic areas of closely allied raags. When a knowledgeable artiste employs this approach, he is flirting with danger, trying to see how much he can push the envelope before returning back to home base.

Ustad Faiyaz Khan, the decorated Agra gharana vocalist, was the gold standard for Bhaumikji. The impassioned gharana *gavaiyya* could add melodrama to a rock collection, such was his musicianship and emotive capacity. Through his use of sweeping *meends*, (long glides that connect notes), and his spontaneous bursts of rhythmic play, his music could jolt anyone who may have been lulled into temporary comfort.

Bhaumikji's music felt like it belonged to that period of music – the *pukaar* of his sonorous voice, his *ucchar* – the way he uttered specific musical phrases of the gharana, and the stylistic nuances of the famed *nom tom alap,* an iconic free-form exploration of the raag using just a few consonants and vowels to build the raag into a majestic edifice.

The small hall was filled with many students and their families, as well as young and senior musicians. I sat behind him, playing tanpura and poised for vocal support – a position I found more stressful than even being the soloist. Concentration levels would have to be on high alert so I could decode what he was doing, anticipate what he would do next, and be ready at any moment to fill in with the phrase appropriate to his thought process at that time. And if I hadn't learned the raag, I would have to somehow decipher it as the concert progressed.

The Desi he sang was reminiscent of a bygone era, rooted in his lifetime of musical love and loss. As he sang, '*Mora man har lino*,' a sense of defeat tinged with melancholy permeated the hall, a heart hopelessly defeated in the battle of love. But lingering strains of Desi's moody afternoon sprawling were soon wiped clean with a sparkling and hopelessly romantic Shuddh Sarang, where Bhaumikji managed to single handedly lift the burdens of life off our shoulders. We were reminded that life isn't all about sulking in the doldrums – it was just as much about joy, always retaining the ability to be in wonder of its beauty.

'Give love to your audience. After all, we are all connected, what is the difference between any of us? Look into their faces and find yourself there,' he advised me when I spoke to him about my own stage fright.

He was seventy-five at this time, and he occasionally experienced joint pain when he sat cross-legged on the ground for long stretches. On stage he remained unfazed, stretching his leg out in between raags. He was at ease, as though he was in his 120 square foot room with nobody else around. He tucked his leg back in and launched into the concluding Bhairavi in one of his favourite forms, the *tappa*. It's a rather glitzy style that features fast clusters of note patterns in dense groups, where the rapid voice movements overlap like ripples, unclear where one begins and the other ends. Rendering the famous *Lalvala Joabana*, his voice flits rapidly through Bhairavi like a butterfly preparing for flight.

Bhairavi signals the end of the concert – suddenly the mundanity of life starts to creep back and our temporary escape fades. '*Maza aaya*,' he says, with a twinkle in his eye. He packs up his things to head back home, leaving the bustle of people waiting to congratulate him, to return to his monastic life as a *sadhak*.

—

The Maharaja of Mysuru, Krishnaraja Wodeyar IV, was a musicophile. It is said that he played eight instruments, ranging from veena to saxophone. After he was crowned king as a mere adolescent, his passion for music would play a significant role in his promotion of culture and patronage of many artistes of different musical styles.

As far as Hindustani music was concerned, he took a strong liking to musicians of the Agra gharana, though he invited artistes of all gharanas to perform at his court. After hearing a recital of Ustad Natthan Khan in Bombay, he immediately invited him to be a court musician in Mysuru at a salary of ₹175 per month. When Natthan Khan passed away, he approached none other than Ustad Faiyaz Khan, arguably the most popular Hindustani vocalist at the time who would become a frequent performer at the palace. As Khan Saheb was already employed at the palace in Baroda, he could not accept his offer to be court musician, but suggested another great of the Agra gharana for the job, Ustad Vilayat Hussain Khan. In his predilection for these Agra gharana musicians, Wodeyar may have unintentionally planted the seeds for a sub-culture of Agra gharana Hindustani musicians in the Mysuru-Bengaluru area.

Aside from the Mysuru palace, Northern Karnataka is legendary for being a rich Hindustani music belt. Perhaps because of its proximity to Maharashtra, and the great deal of Marathi culture that was inherent to communities in cities like Belgaum, Dharwad, and Bijapur. Or perhaps, it was because musicians en route to Mysuru from Maharashtra often broke their journeys in these cities, giving them a chance to share their music and build new audiences. Either way, this region was a cultural hotbed and one more entry point for this style, blurring the geographical boundaries of 'North Indian' and 'South Indian' music.

The city of Bengaluru started to show a more organized following of Hindustani music in the 1930s and 1940s, when some of the first serious gurus, such as Acharya Govind Vithal Bhave and Pandit Ramarao Naik, started to teach many students. By the late 70s and 80s, when Kaala moved there, the community may have been niche but it was well-formed. Bhat Saheb had advised him to continue his training under Ramarao Naik, the Agra gharana exponent in south India who had direct training from *khandani* musicians Ustad Faiyaz Khan, Ustad Ata Hussain Khan, and Swami Vallabhdas, a senior disciple of Faiyaz Khan Saheb.

Kaala settled down in the suburb of Indira Nagar with his family and started searching for ways to meet Naik Saheb. If only it was as simple as making a phone call and scheduling a time to meet. Naik Saheb was a man of a different era with strong habits and principles. A strict Brahmin, he performed religious rituals frequently and fasted twice a week; he rode his bicycle from his home in central Chamrajpet around the city to take tuitions in all corners. Many classical musicians are blanketly described as humble and modest, but Naik Saheb was a single earner who supported a large extended family with only his earnings from tuitions as a guru, for which he never quoted a fee. Students donated whatever they could and tried to support him and his family through many hard times.

Kaala heard that Naik Saheb taught a lady who lived in his area, Shantha Poti. After making her acquaintance, she invited him over during one of her lessons so he could have a context to meet. He introduced himself, gave the reference of his guru, Pandit S.C.R. Bhat, and requested a chance to sing for him. '*Haan haan, karenge, karenge*,' Naik Saheb said, and rode off on his bicycle. Kaala kept trying to pin him down, but each time Naik Saheb seemed to evade their meeting. This rigmarole went on for almost eight months! He was befuddled, but undeterred as he had spent decades searching for a guru before. Like many of the old masters, Naik Saheb was testing this potential disciple's commitment, but when would he decide that he had passed the test?

Finally, another musician friend, Ananthswamy, devised a plan to help him out. He was organizing an all-night concert of Naik Saheb's students – he invited Kaala to the programme and gave him a slot around 3 a.m. When his turn came, he performed the morning raag Todi with gusto, showcasing the *talim* he had received from Bhat Saheb. It was the first time Naik Saheb finally heard Kaala sing after all the months he had sought an audience with him, just to audition to be his student. After he finished, Naik Saheb finally told him, '*Kal aa jaana.*'

Ramaraoji's style of training was nothing like Bhat Saheb's. From a structured methodology, he went into a free form musical exchange. Sometimes classes would be twenty minutes, other times hours. Nothing could be written down during class, no theoretical analysis, no over-intellectualizing of the musical process. He would begin teaching a raag by singing a *nom tom alap*, then spend a short time sharing the composition, and leave the student to explore and improvise on his own. But in whatever span of time covered, he had a unique ability of leaving a deep musical impression of the raag in the student's mind. The approach bypassed methodology and went straight to the emotive soul of the raag. That impact became the entry point from which students discovered a raag. Initially, Kaala enjoyed long sessions with Naik

Saheb, so much so that other students would attend his classes to see what was transpiring. After a few years, however, Naik Saheb became a little more aloof, and it became harder for Kaala to get one-on-one time with him. He never knew the reason for the change of heart, nor did he question or complain about it. As it is, matters in other areas of his life were in flux and family pressures persisted.

The data processing business didn't succeed. Trying to bounce back, the brothers attempted an electroplating business, another misfire. Finally, Bar da was determined that they get into the business of transporting sand for construction sites. Despite several efforts to dissuade him from this, Bar da wouldn't be convinced otherwise. Kaala found it hard to be taken seriously as he was and would always remain the youngest child of the family. They invested in a brand-new lorry and launched the business – a few months later, the lorry got into an accident in a village, killing a cow and upsetting the villagers. Whatever income they had generated went back into repairing the vehicle and extricating themselves from the mess they found themselves in. They tried to minimize their losses by selling the lorry, and finally came to a consensus on one thing: businesses were no longer the way forward.

Through all of this, Kaala had built a sizable student base around Bengaluru – he was earning money through tuitions and contributing to the family's expenses. Still, there was family pressure that he should hold a traditional job that had security and stability. After the consecutive business failures, Kaala couldn't bear it any longer. As Bar da had held on to his job at IBM through all their business ventures, Kaala felt the weight of making the businesses work on his shoulders. Yet, he knew deep down that neither of them were really cut out for the business world, having grown up groomed for academic lives, a completely different skill set. He began applying for jobs and when he received an interview in Delhi, he made the trip in the hope of starting anew yet again. Soon after completing the interview, he received a phone call from back home. Bar da had passed away from a heart attack. Could this actually be true? Shattered, Kaala rushed back home in disbelief that his beloved Bar da had died at the age of fifty-one in his absence.

In a life that only knew flux – the early loss of a father in a family of nine, the destabilizing effects of migration through tumultuous historical times, financial precariousness, and the unrelenting search for some meaning in life through music, one unwavering constant Kaala had always counted on since his childhood was the presence of Bar da.

How would life go on?

The loss had shattered the entire Bhaumik family. Bindubasini could not imagine she would live to see the death of her first born – the child who had sacrificed so many of his aspirations to support the entire family after Jogendranath's passing, seeing to it that each of his siblings built a future of promise. Despite the hope that the childrens' academic successes had given her, Bindubasini's strength continued to be tested. Just eight years earlier, her youngest daughter Geeta tragically died in a car accident in Canada, leaving behind a husband and two young children. Bindubasini would make her first foreign trip to put her daughter to rest, managing to travel across seas and continents speaking only Bangla. And after Bar da's passing, she again mustered the wherewithal to steel herself for her family and continue to be their rock.

While Kaala processed the emotions and shock of this loss, he also had to face the murmurs and whispers in his family that he had some part to play in his brother's demise. People insinuated that the stress of their business failures had taken a toll on Bar da's health. To have lost his brother was devastating, but to have lost the respect and trust of certain family members caused a pain so searing that life was suddenly imbued with a deep bleakness.

'I was a black sheep in the family. Everybody discarded me, they said I was a good for nothing fellow. So, one has to face it.'

He accepted the job offer in Delhi. With Sucheta and their two sons, they left Bengaluru and for the first time, lived as a nuclear family of four. He spent the next year as a management consultant, but deep dissatisfaction and frustration with his life led to an inevitable realization. He pleaded with Sucheta, 'I promise to support you, but please allow me to do music, which is what I really love to do.'

She had the conviction and trust in her husband to agree, so they made their way back to Bengaluru. Bau di was overjoyed to be reunited with her sister, so much so that she made a pact with her that from that point onwards, the sisters would live together and never separate again. Over the years, Bau di had become a mother figure to Kaala just as Bar da had been a father figure. She united with Sucheta in support of Kaala's choice to make music his full-time profession. At the end, the women of his family would be the bedrock on which he could follow the artistic path, facing uncertainty and risk for the prospect of a rich inner world.

When news of his return to music as a full-time profession reached Bombay, an opportunity arose at the Bharatiya Vidya Bhavan at Chowpatty. Pandit Dinkar Kaikini, its principal and guru-*bandhu* of Bhat and Ginde, offered Kaala a teaching position that would pull him back to Mumbai. Through all his years of moving cities and career changes, Kaala had been in touch with all three gurus from his *parampara*, giving vocal support for innumerable local and outstation concerts. Living in Mumbai, whether in the 1980s or in the 2020s, means facing one harsh reality: the challenge of finding an affordable and decent place to live. Kaala had to manage his expenses and send money back home within his monthly salary of ₹700 per month. The test of the true depths of his desire to make a living from music were absolutely unrelenting. Living in a lodge in Goregaon filled with bed bugs for five months. Having to move out of a friend's place because of a cranky mother-in-law. Contracting chickenpox. Developing a hernia after the daily ritual of collecting and carrying drinking water while still weak from chickenpox. Undergoing surgery for the hernia. He remembers these challenges vividly.

'Sometimes I went through the day with no money in my pocket, but that didn't bother me. At times I thought to myself, "If I don't get any place to stay, I will stay on the platform." I felt a lot of acceptance on my part – I said okay to whatever life presented. In fact, when people suggested that I take academic tuitions so I could earn much more money, I was very clear that I don't want to do anything else but music. I have tried so many things, now I will only do music. From this point, I never tried anything else.'

Despite these setbacks, his student base at Bharatiya Vidya Bhavan grew to a robust batch of thirty young boys. He groomed them from the basics into capable young singers, some of whom would go on to become teachers and performers in the music industry themselves. It was a golden period at the Bhavan – students, faculty, and visiting artistes performed regularly and the community as a whole was very invested in the musical culture being nurtured.

His *talim* took on a renewed level of intensity. Without a job and gruelling commute eating into all of his time, he could finally prioritize music. He had a strict routine that would go on for more than a decade: learning two days a week each from Bhat Saheb, Ginde Saheb, and Kaikini Saheb, and once a week from Vidushi Shobha Gurtu.

This way, not a day was spared without learning. After so many years of mining his schedule for any pockets of time, he was finally free to exclusively learn (except for the hours he spent teaching), and wanted to soak up as much knowledge as possible. 'My focus was mainly on teaching and my learning. It was a strict routine, and as far as I was concerned my routine was in full swing.'

Each guru had his own flavour and approach, and Kaala took from everyone and created a blend of his own. While Bhat Saheb was a patient yet stringent figure, each of Ginde Saheb's classes was like a performance. Ideas would pour out, and students were often in the vocal support role – when he asked them to sing, instant replication was expected. He had no patience for repetitions. The vibrancy and spontaneity of his *laykari* in particular, the rhythmic patterns he would create with words or notes, would be a hallmark that influenced Kaala deeply. Kaikini Saheb focused on training the mind – the thought process behind improvising, composing, and performing – in addition to the repertoire itself. When inspired, he would compose *bandish*es during their sessions and have Kaala notate them on the spot. He spent many evenings with him in discussions about aesthetics, musicianship, and the yesteryears of music.

In a completely different musical realm, he became very dear to the *thumri* queen, Shobha Gurtu. Kaala's interest in semi-classical repertoire went back to his IIT days when he was first introduced to the genre by his friend Ranjit. When he asked Gindeji for permission to learn from Shobhaji, he encouraged him to go to her, adding that his *khayal gayaki* would benefit greatly from her training.

Initially, Kaala found *talim* with Shobhaji very challenging. His masculine and aggressive Agra gharana voice throw needed modification while singing *thumri* – '*Aise gaane se thumri nahi banega, soft karo avaaz!*' she used to scold repeatedly. Her music was based in *dhun* and *bhav*, intuitive and fast changing. Students struggled to decipher the phrases she sang, and she would keep moving, ornamenting the lyrics and finding fluidity between raags, making her *thumri* renditions so unexpected. The process was so instinctive for her that she did not think of notes or raag as she created melody – if a student asked her for a notation and Kaala was present, she would reply: '*Bhaumik Saheb ko pucho meine kya gaaya.*' She appreciated his pursuit of knowledge and sent her son, Narendra, to study *khayal* with him.

For Kaala, Shobhaji illuminated one important aspect of his musicianship: 'Music without emotion and feeling is not music. It's just a vocal exercise. The approach always has to be from the point of *bhav*. Because after all, you are not a machine. You are a human being, you have feelings, you have emotions. Your presence should be there in each *svar*.'

Concerts happened on and off – Kaala was not made for the politicking and self-promotion that were part of concertizing, nor was he interested in it. But when he did perform, he received very promising critical praise.

Mohan Nadkarni, a critic whom many musicians feared and respected for his deep knowledge of the art and fearless wielding of the pen, happened to attend one of his *mehfils* on Warden Road out of curiosity about a new vocalist whom he would call 'a revelation.'

> 'Merely to say that Bhowmick [sic] stood the test is to leave much unsaid. He came out of it with flying colours, shaping the raga into an imposing majestic structure revealing his keen sense of style and a keener sense of what is subtle, beautiful and emotional. It had all the musical and rhythmical virtues that are associated with a truly involved performance. To this writer, it came as a revelation.' – Mohan Nadkarni, *Economic Times*, 25 September 1988

What seemed to have impressed Nadkarni the most, beyond talent, skill and evidence of serious training, was the impact the music left on his being.

> 'Above all, it is the intensity of this feeling which informed his four-item fare that deservedly brought him applause from his listeners. The final Bhairavi number... came as an impassioned expression of a deeply distraught soul.'

Kaala's tumultuous life was channelled in his music. 'If you have gone through difficult situations and still managed, it's good. You've faced life and lived life. I call that living. These make you realize so many things about what life is about. And that can transform your music. You will hang on to it with more intensity,' he reflects.

There was a part of Kaala at age forty-nine that was still asking himself the same question he had asked his cousin sister when he was an eight-year-old, 'What am I supposed to do in this life?'

Though his *talim* and teaching had over a decade of momentum after quite a dramatic series of twists and turns, he did not tire of seeking new and unrealized experiences. And when he got an inkling of his next adventure, often he would launch into a deep dive without fretting over possible consequences. Just as he had jumped aboard a train to find Mr Shukla, or showed up at IIT and IIM entrance exams without even writing a practice paper, or changed career paths into the volatile and financially unforgiving field of classical music at age thirty-seven. 'I always kept trying things, without thinking about the future. I never planned anything or thought that, "If I do this, this will happen." I'm not a very predictable person. Next moment what I will do, I also don't know.'

He befriended a wealthy, free-spirited vagabond of sorts named Ravindra. Ravindra planted the notion of undergoing an extended period of *sadhana* in nature, as done by spiritual seekers and sadhus. It struck Kaala's fancy – 'I wanted to find out about the sadhu's lifestyle.'

After eleven years as a guru at the Bharatiya Vidya Bhavan, he resigned and announced that he was going to Amarkantak, a sacred spot in the thick of the Vindhya hills in Madhya Pradesh, at the source of the Narmada River. He and Ravindra wanted to live amongst the sadhus who had settled there for generations.

He broke the news to his family and gurus, and all knew that once he had decided to do something, there was no stopping him. Giving his family all the money from his provident fund, supplemented by some support from Ravindra, he packed up and left for the forest.

They arrived at the door of one sadhu's hut and began their practice. Kaala's goal was to penetrate a deeper level of consciousness in his musical *sadhana* in an atmosphere pregnant with meditation. But for some reason unknown to him, the sadhu did not particularly like Kaala, and the discomfort of this tension was unpleasant at the least. As they searched for more places to stay, they realized that it was actually quite difficult to find a genuine sadhu. Many had set up establishments to invite tourists or seekers to stay with them for a fee or donation. This monetization seemed to somehow cast a dubious shadow on the true practise of detachment.

'There were some genuine sadhus we found, who just go out into the jungle, have a fire in front of them and do *sadhana*. But I saw only very few of them doing it.'

They moved around, staying for some time at the Ramakrishna Mission, and other times at huts that welcomed visitors. Perhaps this turbulence was meant to be part of his tryst with *sadhana*, because within three months, Kaala contracted malaria. The jungle was swarming with mosquitoes, and it was too isolated to access the treatment he urgently needed. His condition deteriorated fast, so he gathered all his luggage and left shortly for Bombay, where two students who were doctors took him in and nursed him back to a baseline level. Once he was stable enough to travel, he left for Bengaluru and took months to recover under Sucheta's care.

'I was almost on my deathbed. My weight became 45 kgs. I was not able to sleep at night, I used to disturb my wife at night saying, "Look I'm not able to sleep." It was a terrible time. Actually, I thought that maybe this is the end of my life. But still it was okay, slowly I recovered.

Some people will say it was not necessary. I don't know, possibly it was not necessary. It was just a phase, a new kind of experience. But I believe I was supposed to go through all this nonsense, and that's okay. In fact, all these experiences have made me who I am. When I went to Amarkantak, I was in search of something. Trying to find some way, some system. But finally, it taught me this: don't run away. You cannot run away and do some *sadhana*. It is possible to be with your people and do your *sadhana*. That is one thing I have learned. Be here. And do your things.'

When he gained his strength and health back, he went back to Mumbai, this time with a slightly different frame of mind. 'I didn't want any further changes in my life. I wanted to be stable.' If going to Amarkantak was his personal *tirobhav*, *avirbhav* was his return to Mumbai, his anchor.

He shuttled between different flats in the Talmakiwadi Housing Society, sometimes sharing with students and other roommates until he could get a single room. He had to build his private student base again as he was no longer affiliated with Bharatiya Vidya Bhavan. But over the years he would nurture a loyal group of people from varied backgrounds, from industrialists and Nepean Sea Road homemakers to playback singers and doctors. He completely threw himself into teaching from morning to night, seven days a week, and supported Sucheta and the boys as they continued to live in Bengaluru.

He had not given up on his quest for deeper, philosophical answers about life, however. One of his students relentlessly pestered him to try the Landmark Forum programme, an international personal development course that can be both jolting and transformative, aiming to empower individuals to yield control over their lives, relationships, and frame of mind. It resonated very deeply with Kaala, and he found freedom and lightness in confiding many long-held feelings to his close ones. He also found great inspiration and spiritual direction in the philosophy of Jaggi Vasudev, and took the courses offered at his ashram and felt a shift of perspective. He believes strongly in the value of a spiritual anchor in life.

'Though it is very difficult to show the connection, spirituality changes your personality. It transforms your being, the way you look at things, the way you deal with people and situations. It totally changes the way you look at life itself. Life is empty, meaningless, and that is the truth. You are born here, live for a few years, and then you die. Does it have any meaning? Absolutely nothing. But you have to create your own purpose, and it is necessary to create a purpose. If you contribute something to society, then it becomes meaningful. And yet, if you know that even all this doesn't mean anything, then you won't be pulled down by your emotions and other things. They will not affect you. Because you know that these emotions and feelings have no meaning either. I'm not saying you should not have them, you can have them. But when you know they don't actually mean anything, it allows you to move ahead. That's how it is.'

Landmark courses are known for their long gruelling days and gestapo attendance and timing policies. Nobody can leave the premises except under extenuating circumstances. He was in the middle of the Introduction Leaders Programme, their advanced training programme, when a volunteer pulled Kaala aside at 11.30 p.m. one night. There had been an emergency call from his family in Bengaluru . It was about his first born, Dhrubajyoti – he was seriously ill, and Kaala needed to go to Bengaluru as soon as possible. He flew the same night.

'I knew that he was no more.'

Dhrubajyoti died of a heart attack at the age of twenty-nine.

'He just left.' In Kaala's mind, his son had chosen to leave.

After decades of loss, moving cities, soul searching, and trying all sorts of avenues of work, Kaala had finally come to a stasis point. 'I didn't want any further changes in my life. I wanted to be stable.'

And yet, the moment some balance was achieved, life seemed to throw a meteor on his plate.

'Death does not bother me because I have seen death so many times. It is nothing new to me. If death has to come, it's all right, I can face it. Even today, I'm ready. It doesn't mean anything.'

At the time, Dhrubajyoti was married and a successful marketing executive – a sociable, helpful and outgoing young man. Sucheta was beyond devastated – she had dedicated her life to raising both her sons and keeping them her topmost priority through all the ups and downs of their family journey.

On his way to Bengaluru, Kaala braced himself for tough times ahead. 'I prepared myself to face these things now. There is no way I can break down. I can't afford to do that, because I have to manage my family. I was quite strong. I went there and faced it. My wife's condition was bad, but she is also very brave and strong. She could manage, go through it. I stayed there for some time with them before I came back to Mumbai. I was okay, but at times I used to feel very sad, so immediately I used to go back to Bengaluru and stay with them for some time, then come back. This went on for some time. Eventually we managed to overcome that shock to a great extent and come to terms with what happened.'

Kaala had spent many years wrestling with his inner conflicts. Following a course of life that was prescribed to him by his family, even if done with good intentions, versus seeking a path of fierce individuality. The deep reserves of time that music requires, especially for a person starting later in life, in direct opposition with the time that family and loved ones expect or long for from their father or husband.

'I don't think I have spent quality time with my sons, which was required. Because when they were growing up, I was going through a lot of struggle myself, so I couldn't give my time to them. They must have missed me, but they never expressed it. Probably they knew that we are going through some turmoil, some passing phase. They also must have accepted it, with good spirit. But my wife was very strong, she managed everything. In fact, because of her, she could make both my sons engineers. She is very strong and because she is quite a social person, she could make friends with any stranger like that. I feel that my wife is truly great.'

I reach Bhaumikji's place a few minutes early, waiting as the student before me repeats *taan*s in the raag Bhairav over and over, trying to find the right position of *komal dhaivat*. The student looks expectantly at him, hoping it would be the last repetition, but no such luck. '*Phir se*,' he bellows. He closes his eyes and listens to each student intently, no matter beginner or performer. He is totally present with them.

As the student leaves, slightly exasperated but also determined to conquer this temporary hurdle, she says, 'Sir, I will practise and surely get this for next time.' She is obedient and confident that this temporary glitch can be solved with a little tweaking.

He removes any hope of a quick fix.

'*Ek* taan *ko hazar baar gaana hi hai.* There is no other way, no shortcut. *Ek* bandish *hazar baar gaake chodne ka.* That's the way it is. Here your academic brain comes in the way. It says, "Oh now you think you know it, so you can stop." But in music, your practice only starts after you know it. In academics your practice stops after you know it. But this is a performing art. For performing, you need to go on repeating, polishing. Because execution becomes important. So, it's very different from academics.'

She nods dutifully, perhaps still making sense of his words. Maybe the full effect of their meaning will dawn on her a few years down the road.

We are about to start my lesson when he shares some thoughts still lingering from the previous lesson. 'Teaching music or transferring musical ideas, it's not a mechanical process, it has to do with transfer of feeling. You have to look at it that way. That means if you can't establish some closeness with the student, it's very difficult to transfer this knowledge. It is not mathematics or history, those are fact based. This is much more than that.'

From his early days in Simul Tala when children used

to come home to study, to the friends he tutored in IIT and IIM, and the classes he conducted at Bharatiya Vidya Bhavan, Kaala always loved to teach. It seems that for him, there was something deeply intertwined between the quest for knowledge and the commitment to sharing this information. 'Right from childhood I'm like that, I'm a teacher. I'm also a student throughout my life. I would like to learn more and more, not only about music, but many other things also. I always feel, if you share, knowledge expands. Because you see, if you share some knowledge, you are taking responsibility for that. So if you are sharing something, you need to know much more than what you are sharing. You cannot create a lineage with half-knowledge. You have to learn, you have to be ready for it. Students may ask questions, and you should be able to face those questions. If you don't know, you should be able to say "I don't know, but I'll find out and let you know." I do that. That is what I believe. When you teach, your own knowledge expands.'

But he acknowledges that accumulation of knowledge alone doesn't make a good teacher. 'Passing on the knowledge is a different ball game altogether, but you also need to inspire students. To keep them inspired is not easy. Even though all human beings are the same, sometimes they come with different mindsets. So with your charm, your love and compassion, you can possibly come closer to that person and still deliver, transfer, whatever you need to transfer. You should be in a position to *enrol* them into what the power of music is. You need to talk to them, know them and understand where they are coming from, what they are doing in life, why they are doing it. And very slowly many things become possible. Through music, you can transform people.'

Over the years, offers from many prestigious institutions started to come his way. He was invited to be a residential guru at Sangeet Research Academy in Kolkata and the Gangubai Hangal Gurukul in Hubli. His former institutes, Bharatiya Vidya Bhavan and Vallabh Sangeetalay asked him to be principal. He declined all these offers. I was perplexed and launched into my questions. Weren't you tempted? Couldn't these have given you greater visibility? In your hard-fought musical career, what had your ambitions been for the performing stage?

'When I was young, I had those ambitions – I wanted to be on the performing platform, of course. But it didn't happen, and that's okay. I am not that kind of a person who will pursue others to give me a programme. I'm not a marketing person. I realized that if you want to be on the performing platform, you need to sell yourself, and I can't sell myself. That's not my nature. And if I wanted to market myself, that would have taken a lot of time and effort and the training part would have become diluted, and I didn't want that. Then I reconciled that it's okay. After all, how does it matter? Whatever material I have received from gurus, I'm enjoying that. What more do I want? I have my own approach, my own way of thinking. I always go for knowledge because I love it, I want to know more and more, and I want to execute those things, try it out for myself. Not for just showing to others, but for myself. I want to enjoy it myself. I am not looking for any pay off. Music itself is the pay off for me.'

I continued to press him, perhaps trying to force competitive, results-oriented sensibilities on a soul who viewed life from an alternate framework.

'Right now, my only ambition is to enjoy myself, have fun, that's all. So many things have happened in my life. If something has *not* happened, so what? My life is still on, I can still enjoy my life, and that's what I'm doing.'

When he declined offers to teach or run institutions, he was clear about what he wanted at that point of his life. 'I didn't want to become a party to all the politics in these organizations. I didn't want to trade my freedom for the sake of money, name and fame. Right from childhood, I have never been attracted to money, my mindset was always different. That way I'm also quite adamant, stubborn. So I was happy with my life as it was, and I didn't want any further changes in my life. I wanted to be stable.'

Normally, the external world may view the guru-shishya relationship as a top-down model. Guru gives, student receives, and the power dynamics of this seems unidirectional. But the more Bhaumikji spoke of his students, I saw a different, more symbiotic relationship that defied this convention. He had invested countless hours in them, but they had also given him the support system that carried him through many difficult times. Looking after him, sometimes bringing him groceries or food, providing company, or simply a listening ear. After several decades of teaching them and living his spartan lifestyle, he went from having no money in his pockets to being able to purchase three flats in Mumbai!

'There are so many students looking up to me, so I never thought that I should disappoint these people. I was quite happy with my life, the way it is going, and my students are also taking care of me. People are there for me, there is a lot of support. Right now I'm under lockdown (during the Covid pandemic), still I don't have to bother, things are just flowing, just coming from different people. All these things are also important, you see. I have developed some kind of relationship with all these people. My future may be over but at least my students' future is still alive, let me contribute to that.'

I scan platform 1 of Borivali train station. People move en masse, somehow floating over a limited space that couldn't possibly contain so many bodies. I'm in a rush because I hate to be late. I'm supposed to meet Bhaumikji near the escalator next to the juice stall, but as I frantically pace up and down the platform I realize there are several escalators and juice stalls. Panic sets in and the platform seems like it could be one kilometre long. It feels like a Where's Waldo exercise as I look for his tall, wiry figure and wizard-like beard. Finally, I spot him – in a saffron kurta, cloth jhola slung across his shoulder. I scurry towards him and have a moment of awkward hesitation in the crowd of commuters before I touch his feet and apologize for not finding him sooner.

We are going together to meet Pandit Yashwant Mahale, the last living disciple of Pandit S.N. Ratanjankar. I was doing a research project on Ratanjankar's compositional aesthetics, and when I asked Bhaumikji for his thoughts on the subject, he shared some insights and said, 'We will have to meet Mahale Saheb for this.'

Mahaleji was a guru-*bandhu* of the Bhat-Ginde-Kaikini triumvirate, and after the passing of these musical pillars and nearly thirty years of close training with them, Bhaumikji never felt like the time had come to put his pursuit of knowledge to rest. Even in his late 70s, he sought a mentor in Mahaleji, with whom he discussed questions on the nuances of raags, rare compositions, and more.

'I need to keep upgrading myself, it's necessary. There are so many things I still don't know. Everybody is different, everybody's approach is also different as far as raag is concerned. So you can always learn something new. From Mahale Saheb that's what I learned, another approach. He would explain a lot of things in ways that other people don't – comparing different raags and compositions and that reveals a lot of things. It removes a lot of doubts you may have in your mind.'

We spend the afternoon with Mahaleji, picking his brain for memories with his guru, discovering those special moments in compositions, reliving past stories of creative inspiration.

Our rickshaw ride back to Borivali station is quiet. I think of how he put everything at risk just to live a life of music. I think of the privilege and comfort I have had at every step of my journey, making over-calculated decisions with multiple safety nets. His life has been a free fall with no safety nets, and he has enjoyed the thrill of the ride. Traces of the pain, intensity and joy of his life glimmer in his eyes, but in his music, it is undeniable, unstoppable. I will go home and remain bewildered about the nature of his life. And he will go back to his room, his home for the last thirty years, a rarefied space where music is sustenance enough.

5

KALA RAMNATH

Beyond Instrumentalizing

MY LOVE FOR THE VIOLIN IS SOMETHING THAT IS A PART of my DNA. The genetics can be traced back two generations in my family to my grandfather and mathematician, S.K. Rangarajan. After travelling to the former USSR for academic conferences, he would return home to five children who eagerly awaited the spoils of the trip. He came armed with LP records of Tchaikovsky's *Swan Lake* and *Nutcracker Suite*, and the motley crew of four boys and one girl would pause their games of running amuck to experience a few moments of peace and serenity. It seemed incongruous to have ballet overtures bounce off the bare walls of their flat in Malleshwaram, an old locality of Bengaluru filled with temples, Carnatic music, and kaleidoscopic flower markets. But the sounds of orchestral instruments, particularly the violin, cast a spell on the children.

In the very same Malleshwaram, a huge violin-shaped

concert auditorium, Chowdiah Hall (name after Carnatic violin maestro T. Chowdiah), was and continues to be a famous venue for many Indian classical concerts. Here, the same family listened to many Carnatic performances where the violin was both a solo and accompanying instrument. The sound aesthetic was familiar, comforting, and what they had grown up with. My mother, in particular, was drawn to the tone and expressivity of the instrument.

She eventually transferred her love of the instrument to me. She enrolled me in Western classical violin classes at the age of five after flipping through advertisements for teachers in the local Yellow Pages. I began my lessons by chatting incessantly with my teacher and doing cartwheels mid-class, but with time, I was deeply drawn into the vastness of this tiny instrument. Soon it became apparent how difficult it was to produce a specific sound that went beyond the surface level capacity of the instrument – the beginner's tone was certainly unpleasant, shrill, scratchy, and metallic. But when I listened to the greats, I saw the capacity for great warmth, depth, and contrast of tonality. I continued to play the violin for almost twenty years, and it would be my outlet, my escape from the world. And though I also sang Carnatic music at this time, somehow, I never ventured to play Indian music on my violin.

After many years of singular obsession with vocal music, I was thrown back into my love affair with the violin when I heard Kala Ramnath live in Mumbai. Within one note of raag Puriya Dhanashri – her first precise stroke of the bow – she unlocked her characteristic golden tone. I was taken into a universe of sound in which instruments become clay in the hands of instrumentalists, moulded and shaped to produce infinite sonic possibilities.

At the age of eighteen, child prodigy Kala Ramnath was set to give her first major public recital in Mumbai. The venue was Deenanath Mangeshkar auditorium (named after actor, musician and father of Lata Mangeshkar), a 1,000-seater hall in central Mumbai that featured many high-profile festivals and artistes. The publicity was extensive, invites sent out to eminent musicians and music lovers. As a young Kala looked out into the hall to see her audience, her heart fell to see only twelve people dotting the huge space.

'I was so disappointed, I have no words to express how I felt.'

But in this moment of tremendous letdown, Kalaji received an early and valuable lesson on the nature of a performing career: whether you have an audience of one or one thousand, you pour your soul into your performance for the people who are in front of you. And by sheer chance, you never know who may be in the audience who could make a difference in your life.

That particular day, it so happened that the director of CBS Records was one among the twelve present in the audience. After hearing her, he offered her first record deal, and her career trajectory gained momentum. 'I have always believed that I have to give my best. When I do things sincerely, my experience is that the audience gets serious with you.'

Sincerity, coupled with tremendous focus and discipline, form the foundation of Kalaji's musical journey.

During the early hours of a typically sultry Chennai morning, T.A. Narayana Iyer would gently wake up his two-year-old granddaughter, Kala, sometimes with a helping of payasam to entice her. Dawn was a critical time to practise music, even for a toddler who was eclipsed in size by her violin. If she repeated an exercise five times, she would get to choose one of the coloured jeera goli candies placed in front of her. His approach was an astute combination of gentle affection and relentlessness – at night he would tell baby Kala stories, capturing her imagination and making her laugh, all while ensuring she gets enough rest to wake up by 4 a.m. and resume practice. In this manner, Narayana Iyer managed to hold the gifted child's attention and begin instilling a lifestyle built around an unbending musical regimen.

Narayana Iyer himself was a Carnatic musician hailing from a multi-generational family of hereditary musicians from the Travancore court in Kerala. He was preceded by four generations of Carnatic vocalists, and became the first in his family to transition to the violin. By this time, however, the court system of patronage had dissolved and Narayana Iyer had to move to Mumbai, where he held a post as a clerk in the accountant general's office. Despite the necessity of this job, music was still the centre of his life, and he engaged all of his children in rigorous training. He began by teaching them Carnatic music (T.N. Krishnan, T.N. Mani, and N. Rajam), but sensing the rivalry that could arise from competing interests and opportunities, he steered each of them in a distinct direction. T.N. Krishnan would become a renowned Carnatic violinist, N. Rajam the pioneering Hindustani violinist, and T.N. Mani (Kala's father) used his talents as a violinist and assistant music director in the film industry.

Being in Mumbai, Narayana Iyer optimized the opportunity to assimilate as much information as possible about Hindustani music. He would often meet with leading musicians and scholars including V.N. Bhatkhande, B.R. Deodhar, V.D. Paluskar, and Omkarnath Thakur, engaging in musical discussions and accompanying them on violin. After enrolling his daughter, Rajam, at the Deodhar School of Music, he would sit in on her classes with Pandit Omkarnath Thakur, absorbing information about raags and compositions and translating this into the most effective technique on the violin. With a naturally inquisitive temperament, he would supplement his understanding with study of theoretical texts and extensive listening to grasp nuanced details of raag structures.

By the time he trained Kala, he had honed the technique

required for Hindustani music and implemented his method of teaching on his children. Memories of Kala's childhood revolve around long hours of practice, meticulously crafted lessons with her grandfather, with school and homework placed in the middle. In his diary, Narayana Iyer would log the raags that Kala was learning and keep tabs on her daily practice regimen – unless she was very ill, she was not allowed to miss a single practice session. When she began, in 1969, she trained in Carnatic music, undergoing the regimen of *sarali varisai*s, as well as some *varnams* and *kritis*. Within a few years, however, Narayana Iyer decided that she would follow the Hindustani path exclusively. His word was final, and Kala's parents gave their full support in this decision.

She doesn't remember her childhood much, but recalls that there was a lot of practice. 'There wouldn't be a day when I would be let off without practice, whether I had tests or any assignments to complete. Nothing mattered. What mattered was that practice should happen, and then all these other things should happen. It was hard. I remember when I was in 3rd or 4th grade, at 8.30 I'd be doing my homework, my math problems. I'd be dead tired and want to go to sleep. I would be studying until 10 and then sleep – I would be woken up in the morning at 4 or 5 to practise. It would be hard to get up in the morning, but my grandfather was very nice to me.'

Everything Kalaji did was monitored by her thatha (grandfather). It was ensured that her practice time was spent with great efficacy, rigour, and focus. Each exercise had to be played 100 times, and if there was even the slightest deviation at any point during these repetitions, she would have to go all the way back to the beginning and start over. 'This type of training was one of the reasons why I could grasp things so fast in totality – the whole thing and the words – the first time I listened to it. It was really killing, but it brought about that kind of intense focus. For me, life was about school, practice. I never thought, "I'm going to be a big musician." At that time I had to practise my violin, and that was a duty just like brushing my teeth or having breakfast.'

Though it is hard to imagine a young child obliging this kind of training, the relationship between granddaughter and grandfather was an unusual symbiosis. Narayana Iyer took Kala completely under his wing, musically and otherwise. Starting from dropping and picking her up from school, followed by helping her with her homework, telling her stories at night to put her to sleep, his life was devoted to shaping her into a musician, all without fuss or force. Knowing that she would follow the path of Hindustani music, he ensured that she learned Sanskrit at school so that she could read the necessary musical texts when she became older. Kalaji's inherent nature from the beginning was an introverted perfectionist – neither did she get distracted, nor did her thatha's regimen allow any space for distractions.

Though learning from a family member could be a difficult exercise in balancing discipline with familiarity, for Kalaji, there was no confusion here. 'Thatha was brilliant. He knew how to extract the best from the student, how to make the student practise with no scolding. I was his favourite granddaughter, and I would listen to what he said, that meant a lot to him. For me, my grandfather was my world. If he stopped talking to me, I could not take it. If he was upset with me, he would stop talking to me, that's it. I wouldn't want to upset him at any cost. He made me love music. He did not force it on me – I have a huge amount of respect and love for my grandfather.'

Later in her career, when she received the coveted A grade from All India Radio at the age of nineteen, her grandfather shed tears and confessed that he had put her through tremendous rigour at a very young age, remembering the times when he would wake her up in the middle of the night to teach her an inspired idea. 'He told me, "Everytime I taught you something, you would challenge me by picking it up very fast. I had to think, what should I teach her next?" You would challenge me as a guru, and you have given me the greatest happiness as a guru.'

After retiring from his post in Mumbai, Narayana Iyer settled in Chennai. Though it is a musical hub for Carnatic music, Chennai would not be considered the most vibrant place for Hindustani music culture. Nonetheless, Narayana Iyer ensured visiting musicians always made a stop at their household, where Kalaji would often play for them and have an opportunity to interact. 'I met Dinkar Kaikini, L.K. Pandit, V.G. Jog, Malabika Kanan. Malabika Kanan even taught me the composition, 'Prabhu Daata'

– I still remember it, though it was nearly fifty years ago!'

The radio was also a huge source of inspiration and exposure to many artistes and styles. At the age of seven, young Kala would return from school and wait eagerly for the programme, *Anuranjani*, which aired at 3.45 p.m. The half hour show featured many stalwarts and became a crucial entry point into the world of Hindustani music. 'I remember listening to Kishoriji's Bhoopali, Bageshri, and Jaunpuri. And Jasrajji's Bhimpalas, Shuddh Sarang, and Gorakh Kalyan. When I listened to these, I felt that if music is so beautiful, this is what I want to play.'

Coming from a family filled with violinists, Kalaji was surrounded by role models, but it was her aunt, N. Rajam, whom she admired the most. When she was twelve years old, she went to Varanasi to spend the summer with Rajamji and family, while also getting the opportunity to experience daily practice with local tabla players. Though her grandfather could provide basic *theka* accompaniment (he had also managed to teach himself tabla), in Varanasi, she had more advanced practice with tabla, focusing on developing speed. Kalaji and her cousin, Sangeetha (also a violinist and her contemporary), would often practise together. A few summers later, on another visit, the cousins would perform duets in Varanasi, Bhopal, and Mumbai.

Rajamji's persona and music made a significant impact on Kalaji during these days. 'I idolized my aunt a lot. I wanted to look like her, dress like her – this big bindi I have is because of her. That's when I decided I wanted to do music.' It was also the dream of her father, T.N. Mani, to see her become a Hindustani musician. 'He was very fond of Hindustani music – he wanted to live his dreams through me.'

However, coming from a family filled with musicians – and all violinists at that – came with its own set of complexities. It was not always an idyllic world of musical exchange. 'I can say this – music is something that is supposed to bring peace, happiness, all the good things. But having too many musicians at home – we weren't talking about music all the time. I wouldn't say it was hunky-dory and a happy family. Everybody was aloof, for different reasons. I don't think I was close to anybody. As a child and introvert, I had no idea how the outside world worked. I only did my music and my school education. I realized I was too naïve. In hindsight, I don't have any complaints about anybody. When you're a child, if everybody, including all the cousins are into music, I think there is going to be some kind of friction. But once you grow up, now we have a good time. We have grown out of it.'

Kalaji's lifestyle of focus and diligence received a sudden shock at the age of fourteen. Following a late night of working in the studio with Ustad Zakir Hussain and Pandit Hariprasad Chaurasia on a film project, her father returned home and suffered a fatal heart attack. Her world was permanently altered in that moment, and soon after she was forced to question and reckon with her musical voice and vision.

This was a time when she realized that she had very little support, and she cultivated her inner strength by adopting a spiritual perspective. 'Right after my Dad died, that whole night I could not sleep. I kept thinking, "How will we live without our Dad? We'll never be seeing him again ever." The next day, when the sun rose, I was sitting on my balcony and I realized, one day has passed and we are still living. Now we will never see him. It was very painful.

'When you lose someone who is really close to you and is the earning member of the family, people tend to avoid you, thinking you might become a burden on them. This is not saying that everybody is like that, one doesn't know, maybe they are also grieving. You never know what it was. But yes, that happened to us, and that made me realize that I needed to find my feet.'

Perhaps this tragedy precipitated serious reflection on her way forward, musically. Kalaji felt the urgency, now more than ever, to have a plan for her future. 'I felt lost, I didn't know what to do. I did not have any support. How would I achieve this? I was so much into music I couldn't think of an alternative career for myself.' At this juncture, she received some jolting advice that made her reconsider what she wanted to convey in her music.

During a visit to her home, it was Ustad Zakir Hussain who spoke his mind. 'After listening to me play, he said, "Who is going to listen to you if you play like your aunt?" These were really harsh words. It was painful, not easy. When he said that, it made me realize that it's true, right?

Now what am I going to do? I'm glad he opened my eyes. And events after my Dad's passing away made me realize even more that I had to be different.'

Kalaji graduated from college and soon after had an arranged marriage and moved to Kolkata. While she was there, she had the opportunity to meet Pandit Jasraj and ask him if he would take her as a student. He readily agreed, and in 1989, Kalaji moved permanently to Mumbai.

In Mumbai, her *talim* and performance with Jasrajji took off rapidly. Kalaji had already familiarized herself with his repertoire and style before beginning her training, but it soon became evident that she needed to modify her technique to be able to follow vocal music instantaneously, without delay and with the most accurate replication of phrasing. She realized the urgency of this issue while accompanying Jasrajji in performance. 'If I had to accompany him, I couldn't play what he was singing without messing up. Because within a fraction of a second you have to decide which finger to use for which note.' Within the first six months of her training, she became fixated on developing a new method of fingering that suited Jasrajji's *gayaki*.

The development of this technique was a deeply reflective and experimental process, driven by a strong urge to replicate a specific quality of sound and accuracy of phrasing in vocal music. 'Usually, when violinists play, they try to use one finger for everything, *meend* and *gamak*. I wondered, how could I play a phrase using multiple fingers, but make it sound like I'm only using one finger? These are things that I explored and figured out. The advantage in doing this was that it gave increased mobility in playing different phrases. I was not stuck with one or two fingers, which limits the ease of playing. Also, when you're playing music which is unknown to you, at that moment you don't always know which finger to use. Then you start using one finger and that stands to be out of tune, because the finger doesn't know the spacing. But if I use the same fingering that I use for that particular note, then the finger knows the spacing. The only thing I had to figure out was how do I play this in a manner that sounds like somebody is singing, because if you use different fingers, then you'll hear the switch of fingers and that effect is gone. I had to figure out how to create that effect.' In this manner of constant self-examination and reflection, trial and error, she developed her own technique and approach.

The process took six months of obsessive listening to Jasrajji's recordings, accompanying them as though they were live concerts. She became so intent on unravelling this technique that she only slept four hours a night, repeatedly playing and listening into the night until she crystallized her approach. She was living with Jasrajji and his wife at this time, as her marriage also began to dissolve during this period.

Jasrajji happened to be at home one night when she

was broadcasting live on the All India Radio National programme. After hearing her recital, he was shocked to discover how drastically Kalaji had modified her style to sound like his *gayaki*. 'Then there was no looking back. After that, I travelled all over the world with him.'

Aside from learning in the hot seat of live performance, Kalaji's *talim* with Jasrajji happened organically. She would spend most of her days at his home, assimilated into his family and doing all of her work and practise amidst other musical moments that would emerge during the day. She would have all meals at his home, often celebrating festivals together. 'I was one of the very few lucky ones, not all of them had that kind of privilege. I was pampered because I was good at music. Both him and his wife have been very nice to me.'

Formal learning would happen in a lesson if Kalaji requested clarification on a particular raag, at other times at the kitchen table or even in a taxi. An inspired moment would demand the sharing of an unusual *bandish* or anecdote from his younger days. Yearly *shibir*s (intensive residential workshops) would take place off-site, where senior students came together for an intensive residential learning experience in which entire days were filled with learning. But for the most part, Kalaji self-learned the *gayaki* by very close observation and immediate implementation in practice.

'He gave me the vision of the notes, specific to raag. For example, you can't say *ga* is in this place, or *ma* is in the place. It is in your mind – music is abstract. In your mind, you know the place of those notes. What I got from him was the ability to see those. In raag Desi, *nishad* is not *komal nishad*, it is slightly higher than *komal nishad*. What is that point? You have to see it in your mind, very specific to each raag. For example, if you take the *rishabh* of Shree and *rishabh* of Bhairav, he would ask which is higher which is lower? Both are *komal rishabh*. You have to be very clear about that kind of note placement, and he gave me that vision.'

Though he was patient and easy-going with students at home, if a student erred while providing *saath sangat* (accompaniment) in live performance, he would correct them right on the stage. 'I remember there was a memorial concert happening for Ustad Bade Ghulam Ali Khan Saheb at the National Centre for Performing Arts in Mumbai. He was singing Marwa, and he kept telling me as we were doing the concert that my *rishabh* was a little higher than the proper Marwa *rishabh*. As it went along, he would shake his head and say, "No, that's not it." Then, once I hit it right, you should have seen his face, it was as though I had achieved something! Then I realized the right place, the right *shruti*. After that, it was embedded in my mind. I learned it in that moment of the concert.'

Similarly, Kalaji remembers when one of her violins had been played so much that the fingerboard was worn down in the area of the note, *pa*. The unevenness of the board affected the accuracy of the note, and Jasrajji would look at Kalaji and wag his thumb to indicate that something was off. On the other hand, when she did something to his satisfaction, he was very generous in his praise and appreciation. So much so that he would choose certain raags in his concerts only if Kalaji was present for violin accompaniment.

Kalaji continued to embrace a spirit of experimentation as she refined her style to suit Jasrajji's style. While accompanying him in concert, she found it difficult to play on his tonic pitch of C# – due to the low range, as the strings would not retain enough tension. Even in her solo performance, she sought a deeper and warmer tone. 'Usually, Indians play the violin with their *sa* on E or even F. That is a screeching high pitch. If I had to play a concert on F, I don't think people could sit for even an hour listening to that high pitch. Then, I decided I must bring down the pitch of the violin. The violin strings kept losing tension and the sound was flat. That's when I thought, why don't I try viola strings? They are fatter, thicker, harder to play. I started looking for strings. I went to a store in Houston, Texas, and first picked up some banjo strings, but after trying them out, I felt, no not this. Then I tried viola strings, and that worked well.'

Aside from imparting stylistic and aesthetic values, Kalaji's long association with Jasrajji gave her insights about navigating a career in music. 'When you sit and travel with your guru, you learn a lot of things apart from music. How does my guruji talk to people who come to see him, how does he talk to organizers, how does he build relationships with people? These were very good things to learn, they cannot be taught. You have to watch it happen.

Guruji would observe small details. I had a suitcase that was worn out completely. Seeing that, he said, "You're going to go to your concert with this suitcase?" He immediately ordered a new suitcase for me saying, "When you go for a concert, the way you dress, everything makes an impression." That was a big learning for me. After that, I started observing how he dressed and what he wore in different situations. He was particular about clothes, how we looked. He would make fun of me – "*Vo to* carefully careless *hai*," he would say, because I always had hair falling on my face, and he felt it looked nice on stage.'

His inputs helped her navigate the logistics of a professional career. Once, when he noticed that she was travelling extensively by train, he insisted she start flying, even if it was initially at her own cost. His logic was that if organizers took note of the fact that she was flying from Kolkata to Chennai, then they would realize she needed to be flown to a concert, not travel by train. 'These are things I learned when I was staying with him, just by talking.'

During any free time she managed to find between learning and *riyaz*, Kalaji would be on her laptop, emailing organizers as she tried to break into various musical networks. 'I got my first computer in 1995. I have to thank my brother for telling me about computers. Dial-up internet was really slow those days, and I would have to stay up from midnight to 3, looking for festivals because the internet would be a little faster at this time. I would scour the internet for festivals happening everywhere, and then snail mail my CD. It was hard. But I guess you value your success better when you don't have anybody to help you or tell you how to go about it. You make your own decisions.'

As Kalaji's style is entirely *gayaki ang* – emulating the voice through the violin – her training was always very closely aligned to vocal music. She was always made to sing the *bandish*es she played and feel connected to the text and its meaning – even while training with her grandfather. Her bowing very specifically followed the emphasis and breaks between the words, maintaining the textual integrity on her instrument.

And while instrumentalists do not always feel the necessity to connect with the lyrics of the compositions they develop, for Kalaji, the words and their *bhav* are critical in her interpretation and expression. 'I feel the meaning of the composition, and this plays a big part in aesthetics for me. I play because I know vocal music. Without feeling and understanding what is being said, expression does not come out. For me, that plays a very big part in my playing. I'm always thinking of the words – that is second nature to me – even during *vistar alap*s in the *bada khayal*. I compose myself, I understand Brij Bhasha, I know the language. So, for me, I play vocal music in totality. It's not just *gayaki ang*. It is complete *gayaki*.'

I'm brought back to the draw of her famous tonal

quality, a result of her experiments with the instrument and carefully crafted technique and sound aesthetic. It is a product of a delicate interplay between pressure placed on the bow, movement of the bow, dynamics, and incisive intonation. She emphasizes that proper technique is critical in enabling expressivity – sound understanding of the instrument and musical knowledge are essential ingredients to emote freely.

Most Hindustani musicians believe that raags are more than a mere set of notes or a particular combination of them. Many connect with the identity, energy or mood of raag at a spiritual or cosmic level. Even the rasa theory of Indian aesthetics ascribes greater significance to raags in terms of emotions and mental states. For Kalaji, raags possess an otherworldly quality. 'For me, raags are like divine beings. You have to invoke them to give you a vision. How do you invoke them? For me, the *aaroh* (ascending scale) and the *avaroh* (descending scale) are like its limbs. The *chalan* or the *pakkad* (short, quintessential phrase capturing a raag) is the face of the raag. Raags have moods, the nature of the raag all comes through the *chalan*. Each raag has a character, and that picture is very clear in my mind. How I feel about the character of the raag and how you feel will not be that different, but the expression will be different.'

And while most contemporary instrumental music features a heavy proportion of *laykari* – rhythmic play and calculation – Kalaji is very clear that her musical style is dictated by the resonance of her instrument, rather than trends in performance. 'My instrument has a greater capacity to express than a sitar or sarod can express. I should look at bringing that out. If I scatter notes on the violin, how much can you listen to that? *Alap*, *jod*, *jhala*, is okay for sitar and sarod, but that's not going to sound good on my instrument. One should know what sounds good on one's instrument. That is the reason why I play vocal music on the violin.'

Ultimately, she believes in creating a sensitive balance between emotionally driven passages as well as moments of energy and virtuosity. 'Emotive content is very important, because the emotive quality in an artiste is what reaches the listener. But just being emotive will not work. You must have aspects of technical virtuosity that you have to display from time to time. If you sing a beautiful *alap*, not everybody understands how difficult it is to have that control in your voice or steadiness in the hand to bring out the slow aspect of *alap*. Most don't understand that this is harder than singing *sargam*s or *aakar taan*s. But when you sing those *aakar taan*s or *sargam* at super speed, they clap, but they don't clap for *alap*. They may feel it, but they don't understand that this is actually where the claps are required, not there. Because this requires so much command to sing the note. How much time would you spend going from *nishad* to *shadaj* in the raag Desi, and where is that *nishad* placed? It is not *komal nishad*, it is a little higher than *komal nishad* and it comes from *sa*. People don't understand how much control you need in your voice to hit that *shruti* correctly, but its beauty is conveyed. If a tabla player plays something fast, immediately there is applause.'

She believes, however, that the onus falls on the artiste to raise awareness amongst listeners about such subtleties, primarily by communicating about their musical repertoire and creative process.

'I always share before I begin. In the West, I try to explain to audiences who may not be familiar with this music. If I'm in India, in the middle of my concert, I stop and say how much it takes to achieve this. It sounds easy, but it is not easy.' She wishes more artistes would speak up and educate audiences during their performances. 'We should give them that awareness. If we don't give them awareness and instead play to the gallery, we are losing our music, which is what is happening today.'

She admits to being a prolific listener, spending many hours listening to videos of a wide range of artistes on YouTube. Her listening is a very active and concentrated practice. 'I listen to Kishoriji, Kumarji, Jasrajji, Bhimsenji, Ashwini Bhide Deshpande – I listen to everybody. I feel when you listen so much, something from somebody stays back in your mind and then it comes out as your own. Listening doesn't mean that I'm putting it on and doing some work. I'm sitting and listening with full focus – for me listening is done with full attention.'

—

As a busy international touring artiste, Kalaji has maintained an introverted lifestyle that gives her peace of mind and space to keep ruminating on music. Before a concert, she likes to keep to herself, quietly going through the tasks in preparation for the concert – ironing her clothes, getting rest, and being enveloped in the sound of the tanpura all day. She doesn't like to compromise on her pre-concert requirements. 'I don't go out anywhere. If anybody calls me to go, I will not go anywhere. I will be at home, or if I'm travelling, in the hotel. I won't even watch TV. I will keep my tanpura on, have a little bit to eat, rest in the afternoon, and shower and leave for the concert. It really affects me, otherwise I feel like a scatterbrain. You're thinking about this and that, you're not in that zone where you have to be before you go to a concert. I need that little bit of peace, emptiness, quiet space.'

She likes to keep a free mind before a concert, without much planning or pre-calculation about what she will play. Sometimes, her co-artistes suggest raags moments before the concert on stage. 'I am totally empty in my mind. When you arrive at a concert like that, the raag and whatever you play is fresh. If I work on a particular raag for one week, it may be perfect, but I may be bored when I go on stage, and the impact of freshness and newness will not be there. When it's fresh and new, even I enjoy it.'

She remembers sitting on stage at the renowned Sawai Gandharva festival in Pune, thinking she would play raag Yaman. Her co-artiste, Yogesh Samsi, told her, 'Yaman? Why don't you play Shyam Kalyan?' And she went with the suggestion, as she did on many other occasions.

Outside of her classical work, Kalaji collaborates extensively with ensembles and musicians across music genres, including the Kronos Quartet, the London Symphony Orchestra, Edgar Meyer, George Brooks, Béla Fleck and many more. The versatility and universality of the violin as an instrument make it an ideal fit for more abstract explorations of sound. Kalaji's approach to such projects remains rooted in her Indian musical framework, from which she extrapolates expressions in a new context. No matter the genre, she begins from her homebase, the tonic note *sa*. 'Whatever I listen to, in my mind I first look for the *sa*, and then try to find what raag the piece we are playing could come under. And then I start improvising. When I'm working with orchestras, usually they leave a number of bars for me in the score, and I'm allowed to improvise in between. In these situations, when I improvise, keeping count of the bars is very difficult because there's no tabla. So I have to work a lot to prepare for this, writing down the bars on a piece of paper, and then listening to the MIDI recording of the piece to create my cues.'

While working on the music for the blockbuster Hollywood film, *Blood Diamond*, she improvised in her style over the chords of the score. 'When there are chord changes, I'm also changing raags, very quickly, sometimes in a fraction of a second. Film scores are challenging that way. It's an opportunity for me to learn. It also gives me an idea of how my mind is able to adapt to this. It gives me confidence that my mind is fast enough to keep switching like this.'

She has also ventured into composition, both in the classical sphere as well as collaborative. When inspired by a certain melody within a raag, she pens *bandish*es. She was also selected as a composer by the Kronos Quartet for their project, '50 for the Future,' for which she composed the uplifting piece, 'Amrit.' Inspired by the raag Shuddh Nat, the structure of the piece is based on the framework of *sthayi*, *antara*, *sanchari and abhog* – four sections of development used in Dhrupad and Khayal music. The piece retains a distinct flavour of Hindustani music, especially in its incorporation of stylistic ornaments such as *meend* and *murki*. It seamlessly pivots between a main melody line and harmonized sections that adhere to the spirit of the raag framework. After composing all parts, the piece was notated and arranged by Western classical composer Reena Ismail.

And while she is open to various configurations of instrumentation and experimentation, she doesn't subscribe to musical collaborations that lack musical intention. 'I do not like jam sessions, when you have six or seven musicians together. This is what is happening in India these days. Indian music is not something that is meant to be played together. It's not like Western classical music that is harmony based – we are melody based. And what are we doing, trying to outwit the other? I have tried, but when I play such music I feel like there is no peace inside me until I pick up my violin and start a raag – I feel very weird. If I play two of these types of concerts continuously, I feel like I'm not in my element, like I've lost control of myself. I can't enjoy anything, I cannot sleep, I cannot do anything. I need to get back to my roots, that is my raag and *alap*. So, I do not enjoy those types of projects very much. But I like working with orchestras, where I get my space to play what I want. I can play anything – an *alap*, with tempo, without tempo, it's all up to me. I find that Western classical music is not something that bothers me, whereas in jazz, some of the chromatic scales disturb me. I do work with jazz musicians too, but I try to be in melody. But the truth is, I can only do that for a limited period of time.'

Her projects within the Hindustani sphere are extensive, having toured with artistes like Zakir Hussain, Jayanthi Kumaresh, among others. Here too, she finds that even while working with top calibre musicians, rapport and preparation remain important ingredients for musical creation. 'You have to understand each other. It's not a competition of who's better. You should play according to your strengths and what sounds best on your instrument. That is how we work. With Zakir bhai and Jayanthi, I have a good rapport. We sit and practise – even with Zakir bhai – we plan where everyone will start. Jayanthi and I are both women who understand each other, we both know what we've undergone as women in this field.'

Kalaji is one of the few in the classical firmament who speaks openly about issues in the professional ecosystem that remain unchanged for decades. She has faced various hurdles in her career, including many instances of gender discrimination that have become normalized in the culture of Hindustani music.

One outdated belief that permeates the system is the notion that women are not physically built to play instruments – they are better suited for vocal music. Another obstacle continues to be the disparity in the professional treatment and payment of women.

'If a man had played the way I play, he would be given a lot more recognition. I've had to prove myself twice over. I don't want to take my name – don't you think my aunt Rajamji has made a brilliant contribution to the violin in Hindustani music? Today where is she in relation to other male counterparts? People do not take women seriously. Even now, I've had concerts organized by musicians where I have been treated badly. It could be my stay, where I am placed in a festival line-up. Placing me before a youngster who is a boy, just because I'm a woman.'

In her experience, unequal pay continues to be an issue. 'I would say, when it's a female artiste, there is not much you can tell an organizer unless you have somebody speaking for you, like a manager. I can give you instances where I have spoken with an organizer and they quoted a low fee, and now when I have a manager they offer six times more. My manager is male. I have stopped thinking about all this. After a point of time, you realize these things will never change. You can keep on fighting, it will never change.'

Her identity as a south Indian practising north Indian music has at times been a barrier for acceptance. 'How does it matter if I'm a south or north Indian, all that matters is the music I play, right? Yet, sometimes people stress on the fact that I'm a south Indian. They make comments like, "*Aapke haath me bahut* south Indian *touch hai.*" They don't know, but they have to say this. Since my technique is different, people want to say it's a south Indian technique.

'It has been very difficult to prove myself in every way. As a woman, as a south Indian playing north Indian music, and even to build my audience. While Maharastrians will go to hear a Maharastrian artiste, or the Bengali contingent will go to hear a Bengali, if I play, neither of them come nor do the south Indians. This is how it is everywhere. Only those people who really love my music, whatever their background, come to listen to me. And of course, I have quite a few Western audiences who listen to me. I would say my audience is around 60 per cent Indian, 40 per cent American. Sometimes it can be 50/50 also. When I play with the symphony orchestras, it's 95 per cent American.'

She worries about the future of this music – the growing changes in the music itself, as well as the numerous problems that persist in the professional sphere. She believes that artistes must take responsibility for the quality of music they are presenting without caving to pressures placed by presenters.

'Artistes are not singing the music that should be

sung. Organizers have told them, or they have decided for themselves that the audience's attention span has gone down, so there is the idea that they must not sing for long. Why don't they try singing one full raag? They don't want to do it because they're probably not equipped to do it. And they're blaming the audience. The musician's calibre will decide if he's able to engage the audience with whatever he gives to the audience.'

When it comes to the recirculation of the same coterie of artistes in the performance circuit, Kalaji directly calls out senior artistes to change the current patterns. 'I blame the senior artistes. Some senior artistes do not want to give up their place. Even when they are not in tune. Audiences only listen to senior artistes, they don't want to listen to younger artistes. I would say that senior artistes should support youngsters and give them opportunities to perform before them. Even if they want to perform until a late age, they can still recommend good musicians or talk about them. Zakir bhai openly talks about whomever he likes, and that makes a difference. Why can't the others do it? Bhimsenji spoke about Rashid Khan, that gave him a lot of leeway. Why can't our artistes do that? Today's senior artistes need to promote the next generation.'

Her efforts towards sustaining the future of Hindustani music, and the role of the violin in particular, are evident in her dedicated approach to teaching. She attributes the low numbers of Hindustani violinists to the lack of musicians who can teach the technique accurately, particularly in the articulation of *meend* and *gamak*. She believes that the violin is better suited to accompaniment than the sarangi, because it possesses a tone similar to the voice, but ultimately the art of accompaniment is a highly sensitive approach to following a vocalist with both accuracy and restraint.

'I can only hope and do my best by trying to teach sincerely. I only teach children. The number one reason is that their minds are like a sponge – whatever you give them they grasp immediately and it doesn't bore me. I need some stimulation to teach. A student who doesn't have any idea about music is like fresh clay, and I can mould them as I want. I'm very happy to teach from the beginning – it's when I have to get the student to unlearn and relearn that it's really difficult. That's why I enjoy teaching children. It's mentally stimulating.

'Just as I'm clear in my mind, when I teach also, there's clarity of thought. I try to make it very easy. Of course, every student's aptitude is different. I have to adapt myself, depending on the person's aptitude and grasp, and do whatever is necessary.'

In the spirit of bringing music to youngsters from various backgrounds, Kalaji started 'Kalashree,' an academy dedicated to teaching underprivileged students in India. Inspired by public projects in Venezuela and Hungary that expose children to classical music, she began a similar initiative in India. 'I thought, why not try helping economically downtrodden children in India by giving them a music education, which will in turn help them in other aspects of their life. If nothing else, I've given them something which will be with them always and made a listener who will know a little bit about our music.'

The programme included free training and scholarships for students from economically disadvantaged backgrounds, children facing serious illnesses, and knowledge sharing through workshops and lecture demonstrations. In addition to Kalashree, Kalaji has developed an extensive web resource, indianclassicalmusic.com, which contains detailed explanations about theoretical, historical, and practical aspects of Hindustani music. Video explanations and demonstrations (by Kalaji herself) illustrate very specifically the subtleties of raags.

'I want to make our music more accessible to people around the world, including the layman with no knowledge, students, as well as full-fledged practitioners and also connoisseurs. I feel if I project the right musicians on this website – those who for whatever reason didn't get recognition – maybe they can get known. It has always been the case that artistes don't get recognition in India, but when the West recognizes you, then you become a big person in your country.'

Kalaji's quest for her distinct musical voice and identity set her on the path as a thinking and reflective musician from a young age. She urges the artistes of the future generations to stand firm on a solid ground of training, not hastening this phase in the quest for fame or recognition.

From here, the next step is to consider the ways in which individuality can emerge.

'You should want to be different, to be you. When you want to find your voice, then you can put your thinking cap on and see what you can do to be different. How can you get there? What do you have to change in your style? How will you change it? But first, you must realize that you cannot be any other person, as Zakir bhai said. I cannot be Rajamji, there will be one and only one Rajamji. If you're going to be who you are, think about what needs to be changed to be yourself. How can you get there? What are the steps? Can it be done only through listening, or do you need to change your technique? You always have to be a thinker, when thinking of a raag, or when you're listening to somebody. You have to start seeing those things, and then work on it. And while a guru is needed to guide you, the rest is yours.'

6

RUMI HARISH

Singing Gender

'EVERYONE HAS TO CONSTRUCT THEIR OWN GENDER. Choose your body and feel comfortable with it. I am a man with a clitoris.'

The first time I heard Rumi Harish's music, I was arrested by the combination of freedom and pain that lived in his music, voice, and being. I have heard Rumi sing a rendition of Gaud Malhar that evoked the musical aesthetics of the gramophone era: direct and unfiltered, open-throated and full of heart. I have also heard his rendition of a Sufi song that created uncanny stillness in a sterile auditorium, and a protest song in Kannada that rallied people from all walks of life against injustice. The list goes on. Rumi has never been the quintessential Hindustani classical musician – his path has always been one of a non-conforming questioner of the culture and hierarchies of the ecosystem despite having been seriously groomed in the guru-shishya model for decades.

In his journey of negotiating and realizing gender, he has grappled with his identity musically, vocally, and bodily. For decades, he has been toiling with his voice, trying to unearth a tonality that belongs to him – a voice that feels like home. In the search for his true voice, revelations about his gender identity manifested and continue to unfold.

I have had the pleasure of interacting with Rumi in multiple contexts: as a musician, as an activist, as a friend. He has moved homes many times, but all of his homes have been filled with cats, often unfurling out of a mattress or coiling up under a chair. Friends and guests are constantly dropping in, seeking advice or merely catching up with Rumi and his longtime friend, Sunil. Their home is an open house and safe haven for many from the activist, artistic, and LGBTQ communities. Though he finds daily cooking to be a drudgery, Rumi is a fine cook, often feeding his guests a hearty meal with an abundance of beer on the side. The walls of his current flat are filled with pictures of his idols: Zohrabai Agrewali, Begum Akhtar, Siddheshwari Devi, Gulzar, Mr Hariharan (a porcelain painting artist), Mr D Vadiraja (sculptor), and Rumi's mother, the sculptor Kanaka Murthy. After showing me all the pictures, he confesses: 'I'm obsessed with two men in my life. If I were straight, I would have married Kishore Kumar or Gulzar. One of my dreams was marrying Gulzar and living a life of poetry.'

Rumi is one of the most free spirited people I have met. I have known him for almost twenty years, and I have seen him in many avatars: as a singer, composer, activist, ambassador for change, writer, poet, playwright, theatre actor, film scorer, and painter. But the thread underlying all his endeavours invariably traces back to Hindustani music, an art form that has been critical in his process of self-discovery.

Rumi's quest is to develop a relationship with music that transcends social constructs. 'I believe it is possible to sing beyond gender. We are conditioned to sing like a man or woman.'

—

Challenging gender norms has been part of the fabric of Rumi's life from a young age. His mother, Kanaka, set the precedent as an acclaimed stone sculptor, a profession in which women were not accepted. Kanaka was a significant influence on Rumi's awareness of gender issues in the domestic and professional spheres. 'My mother fought gender fights at home – she was very radical that way. She wanted to do something very strong that would live with her for her entire lifetime. While many gurus would not accept her, she found a guru who agreed to teach her, Mr Vadiraja. I mean, a woman could learn painting, but not do sculpture.'

With the support of her guru and one of her brothers, Kanaka forged ahead to pursue sculpture against the wishes of her family. Even after marriage and family life, Kanaka maintained a strict regimen in her house that did not interrupt her work schedule, unaffected by societal pressures associated with motherhood or wifehood. All three members of the household – Kanaka, her husband Narayana, and Rumi – adhered to a strict division of labour.

Rumi remembers the impact of this division. 'My mother toilet trained me so quickly that by the age of one and a half she made me super independent. She had put a timetable so that kitchen and house work were shared by everybody. By the age of ten, I started cooking. I would cook anything I was taught – except for idlis, I managed to cook everything else: dosa, chutney, puri, chapati. So, I didn't have to depend on her for food. I would manage breakfast, and she would do lunch and dinner. My father would clean the kitchen and wash the vessels. She always divided the labour because she was very clear that she would not stay inside the kitchen beyond 9 o'clock in the morning. She would work from 9 to 6, unbroken except for one hour for lunch. I used to manage everything on my own. It all ran very smoothly until they could no longer do the work due to age.'

Kanaka was a defining force in Rumi's life: fierce, artistic, and turbulent. It was Kanaka who decided that Rumi would follow the path of music, and once decided, she put her child through the same kind of rigour that she followed in her art practice. While attending a concert, a young Rumi innocently observed aloud that the artiste had made an error in delineating the raag. As nearby listeners noticed Rumi's precocious talent, Kanaka too realized his innate musical ability and took him to Ramarao Naik, the Agra gharana guru based in Bengaluru who has featured in an earlier chapter.

—

Ramarao Naik was a simple man, often seen riding his bicycle around Bengaluru as he travelled to teach various students. As a disciple of Ustad Faiyaz Khan, he had developed a stylistic approach that captured the spirit of the gharana. After agreeing to take Rumi as a student, Ramarao and Kanaka instituted a regimen that prioritized music above everything – school and studies were merely formalities to be completed in between intensive music training.

Rumi remembers: 'He lived in Chamarajpet and we lived in Basavangudi. I would cycle there in the morning at 7 and come back by 8.45 to leave for school. When I came back home at 3.30, I would leave and go back to his house.'

The relationship between young Rumi and the elder guru, seventy-three years apart in age, evolved into a friendship that spanned generations. True to the traditional guru-shishya format of learning, Rumi's learning was an immersive lifestyle, accompanying Ramaraoji to the market, where he would learn about the difference between the various local greens and their preparations. As Rumi got older, Ramaraoji taught him to ride a two-wheeler, and later on, it was Rumi who would take him to his AIR broadcasts or concerts on the same bike.

Lessons took shape based on Ramaraoji's mood that day, his state of inspiration. On some days, he would not feel like teaching, and on others, he would sit for his *riyaz* and Rumi would listen and play tanpura. Rumi's listening and observation skills sharpened as he sat in the lessons of other senior students, including Sudhindra Bhaumik, Meera Savur, and Susheela Mehta.

Rumi recounts the way he learned. 'I would listen and practise whatever he would be teaching the others. Ramaraoji was one person whose teaching method was to listen and sing. He didn't have a set design for teaching – here, everything was freedom. If you picked up, you picked up, if not it's your loss. He taught me for seventeen years with freedom in his style. It was our job to figure it out, there's freedom to understand, no spoon-feeding. For him, the idea was to prepare the voice, mind, and heart. He would say, "You should be able to sing anything, anywhere at any point of time, in any taal or raag. That flexibility will give mastery." At first, I didn't understand this idea of singing anywhere. Later, I realized that this meant to not just sing concerts or *baithak*s, but also on the street or the slums.'

This style of teaching gave students space and liberty to discover their personal voice and style. Rumi remembers the artistes who deeply influenced him during these days: Bhimsen Joshi, Gangubai Hangal, Zohrabai Agrewali, Mallikarjun Mansur. Their music manifested in Rumi's explorations of voice, *taan* formations, and *alap*s. But when someone pointed out the imitative quality of his music at this juncture, Rumi went back to Ramaraoji and asked him: 'Why didn't you tell me I was doing this?'

Ramaraoji's reply was in line with his macro approach: he was not responsible for his students' *gayaki*. It was up to the students to discover their aesthetic preferences and give it shape and form. 'For him, every single person had to have the intellectual capacity to be able to decide what is my *gayaki*, how am I going to structure it, what am I going to do and not going to do.'

But this free-spirited approach to training did not dilute the rigour. Ramaraoji was a taskmaster when it came to establishing musical foundations. During Rumi's summer holidays, his schedule intensified, spending full days in *talim* and supervised *riyaz*. 'You may have felt like you had grasped something, but according to him, you had not. You had to be one with it. There were times when he would lock me up in the room from the outside and give me just one or two lines. Initially, I remember singing just *sa re ga ma pa dha ni sa*, *sa ni dha pa ma ga re sa*, 5,000–8,000 times a day.'

Being one with music went beyond sitting in a closed room for hours. Ramaraoji taught Rumi the art of mental practice, insisting that he do an entire *alap* in his mind without any actual singing or humming. And like many musicians, he urged Rumi to constantly be in the mental orbit of music, whether while cooking or riding the bike. The mind had to constantly sing.

Alongside training, Rumi began performing from the age of eleven, establishing a reputation as a star child. At the age of thirteen, he sang at the Devnandan Ubhayaker Yuva Sangeet Utsav, a reputed youth festival in Bengaluru. Whenever Rumi had a concert, Ramaraoji would choose what he would sing. 'He would guide me for each programme and choose the raag. Sometimes this was difficult because he would choose very tough raags and I couldn't say anything. That way I have failed – my concerts were never "prepare and present" types. They were spontaneous – if it clicked it clicked, if it failed, it failed. Audiences have seen my failures.'

While the regime of training and performing continued, the more conventional milestones of life continued to pass. Studies were mere formalities to be completed in a manner that interfered least with the pursuit of music. Kanaka had a clear plan charted out for Rumi. 'I didn't have the confusion of what to study because my mother had already decided. "Do a BA, but don't bother to study too much, focus on music. By twenty-two you should be set in music, by twenty-four you should be married, by twenty-seven you should have children. And then settle back into music."'

Dutifully and without much interest, Rumi (before his gender transition) enrolled in NMKRV college in a course of women's studies, journalism and English. 'Thankfully my mother knew many professors and the principal. She met the principal and insisted that I be given tremendous flexibility to do *riyaz* (ten hours per day), learn, and perform.' To Rumi's delight and surprise, the faculty and college stood by his mother's request and gave him the freedom to continue his music.

As per Kanaka's plans, Rumi prioritized his music and continued on the professional career track. However, a fallout between Ramaraoji and Rumi for many months left Rumi without an anchor in his life. 'For those six months I lost friendship – it was not music that was missing.'

As he navigated this period of life, Rumi began seeking a new way forward. After speaking to various gurus in Bengaluru, he decided that the best step in the music career path would be to pursue training at the Sangeet Research Academy, Kolkata. SRA is known as a premier *gurukul* institution with a faculty roster that boasts of top tier musicians. But for Rumi, his time there would be fraught with multiple challenges. It was a transition into a musical world that was nothing like what he had experienced in Bengaluru – from a more democratic learning approach to a hierarchical structure in which adhering to cultural codes was given great importance. Before he left, he reconciled with Ramaraoji and took his blessings for the new phase ahead.

Rumi experienced culture shock in the move from Bengaluru to Kolkata. Narratives around gharana were constructed and amplified into caricature. He found that musicians were stereotyped and constantly compared. As a south Indian who was fluent in Hindi, Rumi felt discriminated against for not speaking Bengali. The custom of touching the feet of all senior artistes was mandatory, and Rumi was criticized if he did not comply. He wondered: 'Why do you have to fall at the feet of every senior musician? Can you not show your admiration or devotion as it is?'

His training at SRA very closely resembled the strict and demanding rigour of the traditional *gurukul* model, quite different from the rapport he had established with Ramaraoji. The routine was ruthless – waking up at 3 a.m. for *riyaz* until 6, cooking most meals for his gurus and helping with domestic chores, squeezing in *riyaz* and daily lessons between these responsibilities.

'I went through severe depression at SRA – I was very suicidal. I clearly remember when I went to the office late at night and asked to make a call. I called Ramaraoji's number and asked him, if I don't sing, do you mean to say I should not be alive? Am I born only to sing? That is what I hear everywhere, but I'm feeling the pressure and I can't take it. I am not comfortable in SRA at all – with the culture, lifestyle, the language, the practice, the feudal behaviour.

'When I told him this, he simply said, "There's no such thing, life is to live. Sing only when you want to sing." It was such a relief. That's when I decided that I had to go back to Bengaluru.'

Back in Bengaluru, Rumi resumed *talim* with Ramaraoji until his passing in 1998. After this, he cycled through a series of gurus, including a three-year period of learning from Gwalior *gharana* musician Pandit Yeshwantbua Joshi, whom he had heard in concert in Bengaluru. Training under Bua involved a completely new approach – in addition to the traditional format of repeating after the guru, Bua would also write extensive notations for *alap* and raag *chalan* in Devanagari script. Rumi tried to follow along, though this was not a way he was used to grasping musical ideas at first.

Rumi found his *gayaki* very refreshing and interesting. 'He would insist that within just two *swara*s of an *alap*, people should know which raga it is. You can't confuse people and take ten minutes to establish a raga. At no point should you make the audience feel that you are away from the raga.'

During this process, Rumi questioned if there were any truly new or creative musical ideas left to be expressed in raag exposition. He asked Bua: 'How do people enjoy the same thing again and again, when there's nothing really new? We are just arranging the same phrases in different sequences. What is new in this?'

To this question, Bua answered with a new perspective. 'We all have a relationship to a raga. When we sing, we are expressing our relationship. How alive are you in that relationship? That matters.'

This shift in approach gave Rumi a greater sense of artistic agency. 'I became selective and decided that I can shape my music. Just because you're a musician doesn't mean that you have to sing all the ragas. I made a list of ragas that I have a relationship with, and another list of ragas I decided not to sing in this lifetime. I used to think that each raga is a person, each a different lover. But now I feel it's all abstract. With Todi, I have a very fighting kind of relationship, either it is good or it kills me. Kamod is like watching Malayalam comedy cinema with Jagathy, who's a superb comedian. He can bring out comedy in his speech, in his vocal variations, his body, his hair! Kamod is like that – you can bring the most beautiful expressions in any *swara*.'

Rumi trained with Bua for three years, travelling to Mumbai every month for one week from Bengaluru. At the same time, he began doing documentation work for Sangama, an NGO that advocates for sexual minorities, as concertizing was not a reliable source of income. When travel and associated costs of visiting Mumbai became unsustainable, Rumi again searched for a local guru in Bengaluru.

However, personal circumstances made it very difficult to find acceptance from many of the gurus he approached. At this point in his life, Rumi still identified as female, and though he had not come out, his sexual orientation was lesbian. In music circles, his status as a single female, especially one who worked for women and transgender rights, became a source of suspicion and discrimination.

One prospective guru insisted he get married, calling his mother to try and convince her to take action. Another guru criticised Rumi for not wearing saris in concerts, or bindis and bangles in class. These experiences affected him deeply. 'I was not out at this time, I was only refusing to get married. After that, for almost three years, I didn't have a concert. By that time people knew I was working with transgenders – musicians would ask me, "so you've given up music?" Many male musicians held jobs but they were never asked if they had given up music. But if I worked for transgenders, somehow that meant that I'd given up my music.'

Rumi's difficulties grew from here, rumours and slandering comments spreading. 'People thought I had become female impotent, claiming I had sex with hijras and that was the reason why I was not getting married – because I couldn't have children. What more comedy can you have in life? This is the best way to escape marriage, by saying that I am impotent because I have sex with hijras. I realized this was the best chance I had to get everyone to leave me alone.'

During this time of turmoil, Rumi finally found solace in a guru who accepted him as he was, Pandit Indudhar Nirody. 'The first day I went to him, I told him: people have stopped giving me concerts and they are not teaching me because I'm not married. I don't want to be married, I don't like men. He merely said, "That's none of my business, I'll teach you because you want to learn music. You sing well, that's all my concern." He taught me for three years. That's when I was introduced to a more institutionalized way of learning, focused on precision of the *bandish* – it was difficult after being so free and wandering. My current practice is based on what I believe is the musical need and what is the story I am building. This is how I have been working, with the help of Nirody sir and then with Aditi Upadhya from 2013–14.'

Alongside multiple musical transitions, Rumi's engagement with activism deepened. His work with Sangama introduced him to a world far from the bubble of Hindustani music. He was deeply involved in crisis intervention, championing the rights of hijras at police stations when they were wrongly detained. 'All my friends were hijras.'

A period of working for the Sanitation Workers Union opened his eyes to the intersection of caste and gender, and his preconceived notions about being a musician. Rumi used to collect survey data from the sanitation workers while they were working in the mornings. During these rounds, when the workers asked him what he did, he would tell them that he was a musician. 'Invariably, they would say, sing a song. I would be literally bursting trying to close my nose because I couldn't take the smell of the garbage. But I felt I had to sing, because they had asked. It is a real challenge to stand next to garbage and be able to sing, but I've done it. I sang a *vachana*. How could I say, "I sing classical music, I can't sing here near the garbage?" Could I say, "I have to remove my chappal while singing, standing next to the garbage?" Of course not. That's when I learned and deconstructed my concept of gender, class, caste, all privileges. When people on the street ask me to sing, I can sing – this shows my expertise in music. I don't have to sing in a concert.'

Venturing into different spaces and communities, Rumi's mental boundaries around music began to shift and notions of right and wrong began to dissolve. 'This is when I started inventing funny compositions in classical music like "Ba Ba black sheep." I started making things like this to sing for people. While working with the sex workers, I was entrusted with the responsibility of sorting out fights between sex workers under the Hebbal bridge. I totally lost it because I couldn't scream at them. Instead, I tried creating comedy in music – singing funny songs, making fun of classical music. This would make them laugh, calm down, so much so that they would call me every day because they wanted to laugh for some time. I would intentionally kill Kannada film songs and then kill classical music. Before you knew it, the tension was dissolved and everyone would go back to work. Today they will be fighting, tomorrow they will be closest friends. What was the point of actually entering the disputes? The only thing I could do was calm them down. I realized that music is what I have done my whole life – I don't have any other skill at that level. So I used music to quell all kinds of situations.'

Music was ubiquitous in Rumi's activism. In 2013, he worked in Ejipura, an area in Bengaluru in which a settlement of lower income families were illegally displaced from their government subsidized housing projects. Over a long period of uncertainty, many families were literally living on the streets – Rumi was part of a team advocating for their rights and providing aid.

'One evening everyone said we will do a cultural programme, we will heal ourselves. Lots of people were singing and dancing. I was pushed into singing, though I didn't want to sing. That was my pride – I thought, these people will not understand classical music, I have to sing something light for them. My friend Sunil kicked me: "What makes you think they will not enjoy classical? Sing and see what happens." So, I sang a *dadra* followed by a *bandish* in Tilak Kamod, and a qawwali. I sang for half an hour and there was pin drop silence. When I finished, the entire lot hugged me, like they do after a football match. That opened my eyes.'

Rumi was reminded of Ramaraoji's words: 'You should be able to sing anything, anywhere, at any point of time. You should learn to understand where you can sing and for whom you can sing. It's very easy to sing for people with full stomachs. Sing for people who are hungry. Literally starving. This can be a soothing experience for them.'

'I feel everything is connected to music,' Rumi says, reflecting on the intersection of the worlds he inhabits.

Throughout a lifetime of music making and activism, Rumi has been in a continuous process of self-negotiation about his gender and sexuality. All spheres of his life overlap and inform each other: activism constantly keeps him in a space of gender awareness, and music highlights the connection of gender to the body and voice.

Rumi initially identified as a cisgender queer woman. He had occasional relations with women, and in college, while others spoke about their boyfriends, Rumi knew he never wanted one. 'I never thought of men. I knew I was postponing marriage for the very clear reason that I did not like men. I didn't like the behaviour of men, especially the attitudes of many male musicians.'

'When I saw the toxic masculinity in the activist field, I decided I want to remain a woman for several years. Then 2013 onwards, that's when I really felt it's time that I should start identifying as a man, and show how to not be typically macho masculine toxic. I'm going to be a man who is like me. I have remained non-violent from childhood. It became more clear that I'm not a woman. I decided to transition in 2014 – first, I decided not to do surgery but live like a man. This was followed by really bad dysphoria around breasts starting in 2015. Though I changed my name, people kept calling me madam. That's when I decided I'm going through with the surgery. I underwent full surgery except for phalloplasty.'

But the seed about possible gender dysphoria had been planted much earlier, experienced through Rumi's musical training. He grappled with frustrations about his own voice – he experienced some dissonance between the ideal tonal quality he envisioned and the voice he had been born with. 'I was never in a good place regarding voice. I don't know why I never liked my voice. I always thought I should have a voice like Kesarbai or Aditi Upadhya. This was ideal. But I felt that my voice was never like that – and something was not okay.

'It all began in my childhood. I used to play the male tanpura for my guru. That was also the time I began thinking that I was not a woman. There is nothing like the sound of the male tanpura. When you sing with it and feel one with it, it is orgasmic. I have felt wet several times while hearing the male tanpura. That was the true kicking point for me to feel that I want to be a man. Once I did ask Ramaraoji if I could sing in a male pitch, but he said no.'

Rumi also speaks about the constant aspiration to match the voice of another, rather than to be at peace and total acceptance of your own voice. 'I have always rejected my voice and have sought other voices. That hasn't gone out of me. I don't know why I reject myself. Very rarely have I liked my voice while singing or talking. With my earlier voice I felt there was no texture – it was too trained to be melodious. As a child when I was learning, I wanted to sing in others' voices. I assumed I would have a voice like Jagjit Singh after surgery – that's what I always wanted. The moment you start the hormones, the voice gets thicker and pitch goes down. But I never considered that it would still be my voice. So, this is an unlearning process.'

Rumi underwent top surgery in 2020, adjusting to a new body and way of being. 'My whole chest has come down, it's so beautifully done. The conditioning of being a woman is slowly erasing out. Now I feel more free. The most difficult part of life is to break conditioning in every area, from sexuality to gender to everything.'

'I was halfway through my menopause when I did my surgery. I was also very late in getting the surgery done, so my body has still not accepted testosterone. There were many side effects of the hormones. I put on weight, my legs got swollen, I developed very high diabetes. I had severe loose motions and vomiting for the last 8-10 months. My body isn't able to adjust to the side effects of the medicine and insulin. I have to take hormones three times a day.'

The process of retraining the voice after hormone treatment has been an ongoing emotionally charged experiment. For Indian classical vocalists, the tonic pitch, *sa*, is a position that has been ingrained into the brain and the voice. Once this particular singing range has settled into its groove, a vocalist usually remains there for a long time, barring any changes in voice that may develop with age. The position of a singer's *sa* is their home, a place of vocal comfort and familiarity. I met Rumi several times over the span of a year. The first time we met, he demonstrated how his voice had adjusted to singing *sa* on the pitch 'E.'

'When I was singing, I showed you how I could reach notes in E. That's one voice I really enjoyed singing in. I practiced quite a lot then, except that I would get confused about my *sa*, if I sang without tanpura. That was something very unknown to me. By the time I started knowing E, my voice started breaking badly. I couldn't even hold a note, it would break. Sometimes no *sur* will be there, just air. It is like hitting my second puberty.'

This phase of vocal uncertainty created tremendous turmoil and distress. 'Literally no sound was coming out, I thought my music was over. I became very depressed.' Rumi reached out for help from various experts to receive guidance. An in-depth conversation with Carnatic vocalist T.M. Krishna gave him reassurance, insight, and a short-term strategy: he decided to only sing in very short intervals and give the voice ample rest.

'I did a period of silence – for eight months, I didn't sing. I went into severe depression, I couldn't sleep. After this period, I tried singing again and that's when I realized my pitch had gone from E to C. I started practising on C, but I wasn't feeling comfortable. Not even one note would come out straight – it would cut or go *besura*. I stopped people from listening to music or playing music in the house. I did everything possible to shut off music in my life. It was a love hate relationship.'

During this time, Rumi realized that while the voice gets re-trained, the ears also need time to adjust to listening to this new sound. He describes the process of internalizing the new voice as making it an "insider." 'My ears were not trained enough to listen to this voice, they were trained to the old voice. My voice felt like an outsider to me. It can take a lot of time to become an insider.'

In October of 2023, Rumi received a phone call from an unknown number that he would later call a 'landmark intervention' in his vocal and musical progress. The voice on the other end was deep and gruff, and upon answering, the mystery voice asked to speak to Rumi Harish. Rumi answered, and almost dropped his phone when he learned that it was Pandit Rajeev Taranath, a sarod player who was a senior disciple of Ustad Ali Akbar Khan. Taranathji was a man of musical and intellectual prowess, a thinker, scholar, non-conformist, and unfiltered speaker of his radical beliefs. He had recently read Rumi's autobiography, *Jaunpuri Khayal*, and was moved by Rumi's courage and strength. He was calling to find out about Rumi's musical progress, and would continue to call every few days to check in on him.

What struck Rumi at the beginning of their conversations was Taranathji's sensitivity to his gender transition. Though he had met Rumi before this, he made no reference to this meeting nor to his dead name. After a few months, Taranathji called Rumi to enquire in more detail about his progress. Rumi recalls, 'He asked me, "Has your voice transitioned? You've done the body transition but has your voice transitioned? Have you taken testosterone?" I told him I was taking testosterone and also doing voice transitioning. He then asked me, "What is your dosage?" I was shocked that he knew so much about it.' Taranathji offered to help Rumi with his voice, likening it to a voice break issue he had faced earlier. Rumi took him up on his offer and visited him in Mysuru. When he fell at his feet, Taranathji asked him: 'Why are you doing this? Do you believe in it? No? Then don't do it.' Rumi was taken aback. 'I experienced a very different zone of openness.'

Until then, Rumi was mainly concerned with easing into the lower register of his voice, but Taranathji posed a question that made him reconsider this approach and the fear of his voice. 'He asked me, "Do you want to regain your *gayaki* or regain your voice?" I told him that I wanted to regain my *gayaki* and he told me to keep singing. He was ninety-two, and whether people were around him or not, he was always singing. The idea is that *riyaz* does not mean you sit with a tanpura and sing thinking that I have to cover this or that. It's your free mind which can just go along with several ragas, but you have to keep singing. Either you sing or allow the mind to sing, being engaged in music for twenty-four hours in your head.'

Rumi went to Mysuru for several in-person classes, supplemented with online lessons.

In that short time, he went through a whirlwind of raags including Yaman, Lalit, Puriya Dhanashri, Purvi, Gauri, and Purba. 'He took me through all this in such a speed that I couldn't hold it. I came back and started singing. It didn't even take a day and I started singing three hours a day. The habit of singing came back to me. He brought back the passion of being able to practise and sing continuously. I really liked his approach, the free-ness and informality of it. It reminded me of Ramaraoji, so much so that I came back and took out my old books to look at all the ragas I had learned. I felt I had to get back.'

—

For Rumi, the process of becoming one with voice was equally linked to finding new forms of expression, reimagining and breaking the classical music tradition rather than remaining in its shackles. Through his work in activism and theatre, he was often forced to reconsider ideas of structure, form, aesthetics and context. He reconsidered the physical experience of the voice.

'There's something about singing and feeling your voice as opposed to exerting yourself. Singing *pa*, trying to imagine the shape of it, not just round as we are usually taught. It could be triangle, square – in terms of density and sound. It might have sharpness in the corners like a square. I wondered, why was I always taught to create a round sound? That roundness comes from the concept of melody. I'm trying to take away as much melody from voice, another process of deconditioning.'

Form, structure, and text are also areas where Rumi finds play and different paradigms of expression. Various moments of political uprising have inspired musical experiments. In solidarity with the women of Iran, during the movement of being in public without the hijab, Rumi made free form music by playing with the words '*bikhre mere baal*,' referring to the act of scattering or releasing hair. 'It was abstract to the point that you didn't need to add more words, and you could go on singing in whichever taal and whichever way. In a sense, there is a taal setting and an idea of *khayal*, which we just have to loosen up and make more free. I'm interested in less text and more play around raag.'

Similarly, during the CAA and NRC protests in India (which challenged discriminatory amendments in citizenship laws), Rumi played with the words 'Kaunsa Des Hamara,' as a line of expansion. 'During the CAA and NRC protests, my voice was breaking very badly. But I would sing the words "Kaunsa Des Hamara," in whichever raag – once in Bageshri, next time in Multani. That's the freedom of it, same with the tala too. A cycle exists, you arrange it around *sam*, but you can keep changing the tala. You don't fix the text to any raga or tala, and you take one line and keep on expanding. I feel we have to go one step further. I don't know how I'll be received, what will happen. People find it so difficult to come out of their conditioning. Because I question my sexuality and my gender, now I want to question the same in spaces like music.'

Rumi's extensive work in the field of theatre has provided him an alternative framework in which he can experiment with sound, text, expression, and narratives. He dove into composing music for theatre with veteran Kannada actor and director, B. Jayashree. During these projects, Rumi would be expected to create music on demand within a short time, working from a space of spontaneity and immediate association between words and text.

'B. Jayashree started training me. She made me compose a lot of theatre songs. With her, you could never sit and waste time tuning the tanpura. She wouldn't even give me time to find *sa*. You had to start singing and composing the song immediately. That was a big challenge. That's when I learned that you have to internalize your tanpura and harmonium within your body and head – every nerve ending should have the tanpura, otherwise you won't be capable enough to compose like that.

'And then it just happens. You learn the language of linking lyrics and music together. For this type of challenge, you don't have time to think of ragas. It's exactly like any other language – you sing what comes. If it's not right, you set it right. That's all. It's not that the tune comes and then the words. There's no such process. This was the first time I realized that. I've done many experiments like this. There was a poem about different kinds of doors (*tharaha tharaha bagilu*) written by Mamta Sagar that I had to compose music for. I found it more like a rap, so I composed it like this for Jayashree in which she could use voice modulation while reciting.'

Rumi's musical approach is deeply rooted in the visual – his creative process involves painting an image that weaves the soundscape of melody with the emotional interpretation of the text. 'I think it's all about the picture. For example, if you take any old Sadarang composition, look at the word and the movement behind it. *Bal bal jaaun*, what is that saying? I'm completely infatuated with you. How is it set in that raga, how do you reach the *sam*, all in just one line? When you reach the word *jaaun*, you don't need to sing the rest of the *bandish* for some time. Because there's so much said in music and in the words. They are so well woven together, you can actually see it. I think some of the best composers in classical music are Sadarang, Vilayat Hussain Khan, and Dinkar Kaikini. Their *bandish*es possess a dimensional vision that you don't see in other compositions. It comes from the movement and words. I've always loved language. I've sung particular compositions only because of the words in the composition.'

Interestingly, it was Ramaraoji who had initially encouraged Rumi to explore theatre, specifically to discover variations in expression. 'Ramaraoji always said, for the imagination to grow, you need to know composition and you need to know theatre. Because in theatre the dialogues and songs tend to be slightly exaggerated. These kinds of experiments will make you start thinking about why stress is needed and placed on certain words. Then you have to know where to place stress, how to stress, what kind of expressions are stressed, how much volume to give to that stress. You can only learn these things on your own with keen observation through your ears. Dinkar Kaikiniji used to say, see through your ears, listen through eyes. Which is exactly what I felt theatre was doing.'

Rumi has written and produced several original theatre productions. The first, *Sanchari: The Journey of the Raga Kalyani*, was a tribute to Ramaraoji on his birth centenary. 'The biggest gift he had given me was to make me feel that all the ragas are my friends. Sometimes they get angry with you, sometimes they fight with you, sometimes they are your friends. They are just like human beings. I think that idea struck me, that's when I started writing about

Yaman.' The entire play is written in the voice of Yaman – Yaman as an older woman singing '*Aaj Jaane ki Zid Na Karo,*' Yaman as the love interest of Kesarbai Kerkar, Kalyani (Yaman's Carnatic counterpart) as a 'mlecha' or untouchable raag, Yaman as a lesbian.

'People from the theatre world did not like it because they felt there was no plot, conspiracy, or conflict. People from music did not like it because they thought, how can you keep changing the gender of the raga?'

In each personification, Kalyani is an empowered character, defying gender, patriarchy, and caste. For Rumi, this is not an exercise of intersectionality. 'I don't see the difference between activism and music. My musical choices are not patriarchal, not bhakti based. That's why I feel singing has to be political.'

In his play *Freedom Begum*, Rumi was inspired to recreate the world of a *tawaif* from Hyderabad who settled in Bengaluru. Though the historical accuracy of the Begum's existence is unclear, the oral histories and nostalgia surrounding her larger-than-life personality compelled Rumi to investigate further. 'We don't know much about her. She fell in love with Muzaffar Ali, and she shifted to Bengaluru after becoming his keep. He gave her an entire mahal for herself, believed to be in Ulsoor near Hotel Conrad. If people who didn't have a house came and asked her for help, she would give a 10 x 10 space for them to sleep. Apparently, there were 150–200 tenants like that. This is hearsay and nostalgia, there is no proof for this. We walked through that area on a daily basis to speak to many people. We found out about the existence of this mahal through a Kothi who was going to that space to learn about cross-dressing and dance, otherwise she would never get a chance. We heard more stories from people on the streets – all the chaiwalas, auto drivers, puncture walas, beggars. They told us of the Begum's son, who was very feminine and used to dance like her in the mahal. We heard many stories about how the Begum and son died, and finally the whole property got burned.'

Using the information gathered through fieldwork, Rumi, along with Sunil Mohan and Radhika Raj, began recreating and filling in the story of *Freedom Begum*, featuring the same characters they had encountered in their research process and foregrounding inclusivity in the narrative. The same cobblers and puncture walas told the stories of this iconic Begum in Kannada, filled with music entirely composed by Rumi.

Rumi's theatre work has always centred issues of gender, sexuality and caste. In his play *Musical Chairs*, characters rotate chairs as they tell stories about identity and sing Malayalam folk music. In another production, *Love Letters*, inspired by novelist Amrita Pritam, lovers never meet but communicate by sending each other letters. Rumi incorporated a multi-Indian-language letter exchange and composed musical interludes between the sharing of each letter. In *From A to E*, a monologue, Rumi chronicles his journey with gender and voice through his transition, revisiting his past and sharing the challenges of a voice in change.

Rumi's journey of self-discovery continues through various artistic processes. His flat is filled with paintings he has been working on – visual art is a new creative outlet. His paintings find expression for deconstructed and reconstructed bodies and genders. His voice continues to be a self-revealing process, and his style, though firmly grounded in Hindustani, is an evolving exploration of the interplay of voice and text. After a lifetime of body dysphoria, he is finally at ease.

'This is my new body and I'm comfortable with it. I always liked my clitoris. Someday, I want to sing from my clitoris. I'm currently writing my sexual biography, because that is something I really want to talk about – why I don't want a penis, and why I want a clitoris, being a man.'

The process of transitioning gender brought new and unexpected understandings of sexuality. 'Now my orientation has become homosexual. Earlier I explored being queer, now I feel I am a man, and I want to have sex with men. This is something new I'm going through now, I have attractions only for transmen and men. I don't feel attracted to women like I used to earlier because I think the moment my gender concept changed, my attraction also changed. I've been dealing with this shock in my life, it's all very new. I feel like this second life is something that is comfortable, and now I want to explore and train my voice very differently.'

'I believe it is possible to sing beyond gender. What makes us think that thick voices are masculine and thin voices are feminine? What about Mansur? Abdul Karim Khan? I feel his voice is more melodious than Lata Mangeshkar. I don't understand these differences, and I feel this concept of melodiousness is Western. If you compare Siddheshwari Devi and Begum Akhtar, who would you call melodious? Or so many others – Pattammal, MLV, MS, Gauhar Jaan, Rasoolan Bai. Every voice was so different. The idea of a melodious female voice was created to please men, make men feel comfortable. I think male gaze and male audienceship have influenced a lot of the tradition. In masculine voices we see a lot of density – there's no need for that kind of density at all spaces, a thick sound to show machoness. I feel it's very artificial.'

What does the future of classical music look like for the marginalized?

'I don't think the world is ready for transgender classical singers. They're not ready to listen to new kinds of voices.' But Rumi's efforts to bring music to different communities and spaces continues unabated. 'I want to make some kind of cultural capital for queer and trans people in music and poetry.'

In a recent concert in Heggodu, Karnataka, I sang an Akka Mahadevi poem tuned by Rumi. I've had the opportunity to learn several of Rumi's musical arrangements – poems of Maluk Das, Basavanna, Akka Mahadevi. The poem I presented here, '*Chilimili Endoduva Gili Galira*,' captures Akka's wandering spirit as she traverses lakes and caves, communing with all the creatures of nature. Rumi's musical imagination transforms this search into a quest for longing, desire and surrender. While it appears that the text is tuned to the raag Sohini, Rumi's musical ingenuity features a note outside of the raag in the refrain line, '*Neevu kaanire*, (Don't you know?)'. The unexpected weight of *Shuddh Madhyam* drops mid-phrase like an anchor, creating a pause of gravitas that transforms Akka's search from anxious *sringar* to inner seeking. Whenever I perform this poem, I think of Rumi. I wonder how he created this musical moment, filled with beauty and stillness, lyricism and movement. I feel his presence in the melody. I believe he has already created a corpus of cultural capital for queer and trans people that will continue to evolve through his exploration of voicing gender.

Ustad Ali Akbar Khan teaching his young son, Alam, at their home in San Anselmo, California.

Alam and Khan Saheb sharing a moment in their Kolkata home, 2003.

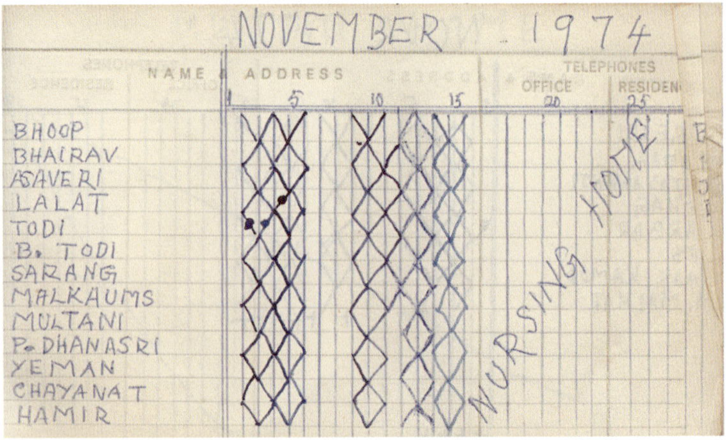

Kala Ramnath's practice diary, maintained by her grandfather, T.A. Narayana Iyer.

Kala Ramnath, age 4.

Kala Ramnath in a lesson with her grandfather, T.A. Narayana Iyer.

Rumi Harish with his guru, Ramarao Naik. Bengaluru.

Rumi Harish in concert, Bangalore International Centre.

Shubhada Paradkar in concert with her guru, Pandit Gajananbua Joshi. Dadar, Mumbai, 1992.

Shubhada Paradkar in Aurangabad, 2024.

Shubha Joshi performing at the Sawai Gandharva Bhimsen Mahotsav, Pune, 1991.

Shubha Joshi with her guru, Vidushi Shobha Gurtu, at the University of Mumbai Clubhouse, 1978.

Shobha Gurtu in concert at the Income Tax Office, Mumbai, 1975. She is accompanied on tabla by Narayanrao Indurkar, on harmonium by Purushottam Walawalkar, and on tanpura and vocal support by Shubha Joshi.

Sudhindra Bhaumik with wife, Sucheta.
Worli Sea Face, Mumbai, 1974.

Sudhindra Bhaumik in concert. Bengaluru, 2014.

Suhail Yusuf Khan with Indo-Welsh band Khamira in Wales, January 2020, while recording for their sophomore album *Undod/Unity* (2023).

Suhail Yusuf Khan at the India Habitat Center, New Delhi, while performing with Advaita, 2013. Photo by Shiv Ahuja.

Yogesh Samsi taking blessings from his guru, Ustad Alla Rakha Qureshi on Qureshi's birthday. Mumbai, 29 April 1999.

Yogesh Samsi and Ustad Zakir Hussain in concert. Mumbai, 2004.

Yogesh Samsi accompanying his father, Pandit Dinkar Kaikini. Sudhindra Bhaumik is on tanpura and vocal support. Mumbai, 1999.

Photos on this page by Rajani Kapse.

7

SUHAIL YUSUF KHAN

Caste, Music, and Society

FINDING A SARANGI PLAYER IN CONNECTICUT – AN American state filled with mansions of hedge fund managers, picket white fences, and Audis – is about as unusual as finding a French horn player in Uttar Pradesh. Yet, on one visit to the US, I was delighted to learn about a sarangi artiste living in New Haven, Connecticut, a college town known for being home to Yale University. His name was Suhail Yusuf Khan, and our first meeting was for a video recording for YouTube. Suhail had a very sophisticated Delhi-ness to him – the grace and refinement with which he spoke, his impeccable attire from juttis to shawl, and above all, an immediate sense of affability. When we began playing, the sound of his sarangi wrapped us in the blanket of an intimate *mehfil*, adding warmth and life to the otherwise sterile recording studio. We were in a typically bland American suburb, but it felt like we were in Lucknow, circa 1940.

I was nervous to perform with a musician from such a celebrated family of hereditary musicians: Suhail is the grandson of the celebrated sarangiya, Ustad Sabri Khan, who was the recipient of many prestigious honours including the Padma Bhushan and Sangeet Natak Akademi awards. Sabri Khan Saheb was featured on the Indian postage stamp, and established his career as a leading accompanist of All India Radio for two decades, playing with artistes from a golden era of Hindustani music in which just one day of radio broadcasts could include performances by Ustad Bade Gulam Ali Khan, Pandit D.V. Paluskar, and Ustad Amir Khan. Khan Saheb himself learned sarangi in Moradabad from his father, Ustad Chaju Khan, his grandfather Ustad Haji Mohammed Khan, and his uncle Ustad Laddan Khan. Khan Saheb's sons and grandsons were all trained musicians – Suhail grew up in a household surrounded by music and professional musicians.

The very early days of Suhail's life were divided between his hometown of Kashipur, and Delhi, where Sabri Khan Saheb (Suhail's maternal grandfather) lived. Kashipur, is a smaller satellite city – previously a royal region for the Himalayan Kumaon princes, and an often visited summer site by British officers who frequented the summer capital of Nainital. This is all to say that Kashipur had a system of patronage and art, sometimes featuring courtesans and other musicians who cultivated a culture of music at the behest of the local raja. The Mirasi community – an Islamic caste of musicians, dancers, and performers –

were given tracts of land by the princes to sustain their art. Suhail's paternal grandfather, Mazhar Hussain, was a sarangi player who settled in Kashipur during this period of activity. However, soon after Indian Independence, and the disappearance of the feudal order, the local patronage systems collapsed and there was a lack of opportunities to sustain music as a livelihood. The town did not have the basic amenities a musician would require to survive, like a radio station to broadcast performances or a local school where they could teach music. Sadly, none of Mazhar Hussain's children took to music as a profession, though they were trained. Suhail's father, Aaqil Yusuf, was initially obsessed with Amitabh Bachchan and harboured dreams of becoming a Bollywood actor. Instead, he ended up learning tailoring and becoming a fashion designer for men's formal wear. After running a shop in Kashipur, he moved to Saudi Arabia in the early 1990s, where he worked in a boutique for almost two decades, shuttling to and from India. Suhail's elder uncle worked as an administrator for the UP interstate bus service, and his younger uncle also took to fashion and became a successful designer. By the time Suhail was born, music was virtually absent from Kashipur, both from a lack of suitable infrastructure as well as inherited stigma and bias against practitioners hailing from the Mirasi community.

Suhail remembers this bias well, a prejudice that was present both internally and externally to his community. 'The very first time I had experienced the pejorative or derogatory use of the term Mirasi in action was in

Kashipur. Interestingly, it did not come from an outsider – it came from our community. It wasn't directly stated to us, but it was discussed in a way that we are "*gaane bajaanewale*," we are Mirasis, while they are Julahas – weavers. Ours was a neighbourhood of different castes and professions.'

By the age of six, Suhail's mother, Farzana Yusuf, decided to move with her two sons to Delhi so that they could live with her father and brothers and immerse in an atmosphere of *talim* and music making. Perhaps it was a combination of her maternal and musical instincts that led her to Delhi, preventing her sons from missing the opportunity of receiving their musical legacy. 'She saw that I had some inclination and interest. I would react to music differently than other children, and she sensed it. I was obsessed with the sarangi, the way it produces this ethereal sonorous sound. My mum tells me that when I was six or seven months old, other children would wake up when the sarangi was played, but I would remain asleep or become very calm.'

Sabri Khan Saheb's house was a hub of musical activity, bustling with his sons, grandchildren, relatives, students, and many other musicians who would often drop in. In addition to sarangi, family members played the santoor, tabla, harmonium, and sang. It was a cauldron of musical emotions – competitiveness and bullying coexisting with love and support. And while each member tried to outshine the other, he would also help his kin in a time of need, after which the spirit of competition would resume.

As a child, Suhail remembers fiddling around with the many instruments that were found at home on his own, copying how others played, and eventually accompanying people instinctively. His formal training in sarangi began at the age of seven, when he underwent the *ganda bandhan* ceremony. The ceremony marked his formal initiation into training, a ritual heavily laden with symbolism, loyalty, and lineage. 'The idea is the concept of *taasir* and blessings. When you're tying the *ganda* on the shishya's right arm – even if there has been involvement with the shishya before that – once it is tied, the ancestors also get involved. You're getting attached to the lineage in a formal, ritualistic manner. The ceremony involves inviting other musicians as witnesses to the moment. In case the student claims in the future that the material is learned somewhere else, the presence of authorities of other gharanas during the ceremony is important.'

A *ganda bandhan* ceremony is also the time when a guru makes a public pronouncement of the shishya's talent and potential. It is accompanied by a small performance, an informal debut of sorts. Suhail remembers having two *ganda bandhan* ceremonies. The first marked his commencement in training, and the second, at the age of fourteen, was a showcase of his talent and potential. *Ganda bandhan* rituals were so common at his grandfather's house that it is blurry in his memory. By the time Khan Saheb had reached his 70s, teaching became his musical mission, and students ranged from locals to family members to foreign ethnomusicologists. 'There were so many students, I was just one on the line. At that time, there was a *ganda bandhan* every three to four months. My grandfather had already achieved a lot, and he was cutting down on performances. He wanted to teach. There were a lot of people who wanted to learn from him.'

Despite largely being symbolic, the act of engaging in the ceremony instils an air of seriousness around training, commitment, and achievement. 'When the *ganda bandhan* ceremony happens, your perception changes and you realize what it takes to be a sarangi player. At that point, I thought, what have I gotten into?'

The early days of Suhail's *talim* could hardly be romanticized. After tying the ceremonial thread, Sabri Khan gave Suhail his first official lesson and then set him off on his own. Khan Saheb did not have the interest or mind space to teach his seven-year-old grandson the basics of sarangi, especially when he was inundated with advanced students. It was Suhail's mama (maternal uncle) and respected sarangiya, Kamal Sabri, who trained him for many years in the foundational techniques that are crucial in a sarangi player's development. Initially, Suhail's young physique could barely manage to sit upright and hold the instrument. But with the careful guidance of Kamal Sabri, who was in his mid-20s at that time and flourishing in his own musical journey, Suhail gained insight into his uncle's musical experiments at a young age.

He clearly remembers this process of learning. 'My mama did an amazing job of taking me through a very technical and difficult phase of sarangi playing, where the body starts to retaliate. Especially being a child, he guided me in the way you balance the bow and *gatta* among other things. His idea of technique was very clear, and I benefited from that. He was thriving on practices which may not have been of interest to a lot of older generation teachers. He was giving me techniques which were overwhelming for my age, but he believed I could do it. For example, when you accompany a female singer, there is a modal shift one has to do. Your *pa* becomes *sa*, and your main *sa* becomes *pa*. That tuning is called *taat mei milana*. It is one of the most difficult styles of playing because the intonation changes and spacing between the notes changes because it is a fretless instrument. He gave me that at an age where the basics were still not clear, and I probably wasn't ready. But having gone through that at that age made me ready for what was about to come. The rest was experiential.'

His days flowed between music, school, and some activities that would resemble an otherwise normal childhood routine. After waking up, he would play sarangi for a short while, cultivating the practice of being with the instrument soon after rising. But he was encouraged to engage in physical activities – sport and play were important in keeping the body in shape, but also the mind in balance. 'Get up, play sarangi, go to school, come back, play sarangi, sleep, wake up, do something else, play sarangi, do homework, sleep. Sometimes I would come back from school, change and go for a concert. This would involve helping my uncles, carrying their instrument cases, travelling with them. I learned so much from that.' As Kamal Sabri was busy concertizing, Suhail's *talim* would revolve around his availability. He would sit with him whenever he practiced – sometimes this would lead to technique practice, repetition of *palta*s (note patterns), or merely listening to what his uncle was practising at the time. After he had developed a sound understanding of tuning and technique, and was confident to navigate a few raags, Suhail was ready to interface with his grandfather directly.

The period leading up to this moment was an uphill battle filled with tests, and Suhail did not receive any preferential treatment as a grandson. 'Even after I expressed my desire to learn from my grandfather, I was tested for a very long time – for years. Am I worthy enough, serious enough, do I deserve it, can I earn it?' The first test was to demonstrate a long-term commitment to the instrument. Many students came and left, overwhelmed by the training. And while technical proficiency is an important part of the journey, Khan Saheb emphasized the importance of *sangat*, or vocal accompaniment. '*Sangat* is actually the overall real *talim* for sarangi players. It is challenging to go through the process, grasp the information in the moment, and absorb that experience. You have to kill your ego and look at the bigger picture – that's not everyone's cup of tea.' Those who endured the initial rigours of training would advance to experience the live learnings of *sangat*.

Unlike the fluid structure of training with his uncle, *talim* with his grandfather followed a strict regimen. After rising early for morning namaz, Khan Saheb would ask Suhail to make his chai, followed by a lesson. After some rest, he would again eat something and resume for another sitting. His day was a sequence of rest, food, and music, repeating until dinner. Post-dinner, students would relax with him, massaging his legs, listening to stories from the past. Sometimes they would go off on their own to practise, other times they would have group listening sessions and discussions.

The more Suhail advanced, the more his grandfather wanted to spend time with him, planning specific ideas to share, raags and compositions to discuss, bow techniques to examine. In his *talim*, Sabri Khan Saheb would demonstrate his ideas vocally rather than playing his sarangi – at this age, he was too frail to play. *Talim* centred around compositions, the entry point into any raag. '*Bandish mei raag hai*,' he would insist, teaching many *bada khayal*s that revealed raag phrases and movement. He was uninterested in typical theoretical tools like *aroh* and *avaroh* (ascending and descending scale), *vadi* and *samvadi* (dominant and sub-dominant notes). Instead, he was concerned with capturing the quintessential phraseology that evoked the raag.

'When he was teaching a group of us Marwa, he asked us, "*Kis raag ki rikhabh* (also known as *rishabh*) *puri hai* – where *rikhabh* is used in its full shape, action, and energy?" We had no idea. He revealed that Marwa is the raag that has *rikhabh* in its full element. We weren't ready for it, but it stayed with me. If that's the understanding you have, you will not get scared of the *rikhabh* of Marwa, which is otherwise so deadly, so scary. Similarly, he said that Puriya's *madhyam* is akin to a heart sinking in pain. These are the small things that stayed with me and helped me navigate the raag web, which becomes so difficult for people to go through. At that time I didn't understand, but what he was doing was demystifying raags for us as people, as faces, shapes, fragrance, so that we would have an easy time to navigate them.'

Khan Saheb had always encouraged an intellectual curiosity about music, tracing back to his long-standing affiliation with ethnomusicologists since 1969. Academics frequented his home for discussions, and the celebrated Hindustani music scholar Dan Neuman invited him to be a visiting professor at the University of Washington. 'He loved discourse, disagreements, perceptions. He was not dogmatic,' Suhail remembers.

Saath sangat – the art of accompaniment – is not something that is explicitly taught, for both tabla players and sarangiyas. Khan Saheb was one of the few sarangi players who rose to popularity and fame because of his expertise in accompaniment, as opposed to others who established themselves while reviving the solo tradition. He would insist that a sarangi player earned his stamp of achievement only when he could play with vocalists from four different gharanas in depth. Whereas a soloist could master four raags and spend a lifetime exploring those in concert, *sangat* requires mastery of numerous raags, taals, and deep and sensitive listening.

Suhail explains his understanding of this process of mastering. 'Presence of mind really comes into the picture: listening, playing, and accommodating to what is needed. Putting your ego aside, working towards making the performance beautiful, so it reaches a level that is unimaginable. That is why accompanists are needed. The idea of having accompanists is to involve and include different energies that elevate the performance. He used to tell us to listen, play, and be so present and available that you are playing your heart out and not disturbing the soloist, but inspiring. There should be inspiration involved. Our *talim* for accompaniment was to study the mannerisms, etiquettes, and social behaviour of the vocalist to understand what they are in the mood for. Unless you sit with a vocalist and tune your instrument, you cannot become a *sangatkar*.'

Perhaps one of the challenges of coming from a family of hereditary musicians is that autonomy has to be earned, and that comes after putting in a period of dues. At the age of eleven, Suhail gave his first public performance in Liverpool while on a one and half month tour of the UK with his grandfather and uncle. At the time, there was a popular trend of musical families presenting three generations of artistes. During these performances, the format was fixed. Kamal Sabri would begin by presenting a raag, Sabri Khan Saheb would then perform a larger raag rendition and a *thumri*, followed by a ten-minute *bandish* presentation by Suhail, and concluding with a *dhun* presented by all of them together.

'I just wasn't ready. The pressure was immense. Also, I don't think it's a good idea to take an eleven-year-old abroad on tour without their parents – a child is not ready. If you go with your father, that's different. But, as a nephew, or maternal grandchild who is one of many – it's not worth it. Touring with family members was horrible. I was scared, I was scolded, I was made to learn things I was not ready for. The stage phobias and anxieties were far too overwhelming for an eleven-year-old child. Musically, I only had material ready enough to play for ten minutes. I would play a Yaman *bandish* for ten minutes. Though I learned a lot, it was difficult. I did not like it, and it messed up things in my mind a bit. For many years after that my confidence was broken – I went from being an extrovert to an introvert. It wasn't good for my mental health, but at the time, people around me didn't have that kind of awareness. Now people do, even hereditary musicians. But at that time, they didn't.'

After this experience, Suhail experienced a deep change of heart about pursuing sarangi as a profession. Though he continued his training and practice, occasionally giving smaller recitals, somewhere in his mind he had let go of the dream of becoming a sarangi player. Interestingly, he started to reconnect with his musical side in new contexts.

In the early 2000s, through friendships and larger circles, he met non-Hindustani musicians from the Delhi music scene. Guitarists, western singers, choirs – he crossed paths with many, and started to explore other forms of music, other ways of making music, and the way the sarangi could inhabit these spaces. This world was so far from the one he had seen thus far: mainstream popularity, fan following, a certain 'coolness' factor.

'I was a scrawny looking teenage boy hitting puberty, playing this old looking instrument. I had no confidence. I was dealing with impostor syndrome. In the family you are constantly reminded of how awful you are – I was very slow. There were these amazing sharp students who would learn *sthayi* and *antara* at the blink of an eye. I would still struggle; I was not doing well in competitions. But in this world, these musicians found something cool in me and made me realize the treasure trove I was sitting on. By virtue of these interactions, my stage phobia and anxiety got checked. It was my interaction with non-hereditary musicians – these normal upper middle-class citizens of India from non-musical backgrounds – that made me realize how normal it is to be who I am. I owe part of my personality to them – I am what I am because of them.'

Though he had interactions with several bands, Suhail's collaboration with the band, Advaita, created the greatest impact on his musical growth. Raag-based songs floated above bass lines and grooves. The dynamic of the eight-piece band was very different from the traditional musical hierarchy he was accustomed to – musical and creative decisions were democratic and cohesive. Suhail began composing a more structured format for the band. Though there was space for jamming within a song, the structure was fixed and the band has been known for their iconic songs. The sarangi was not a token ingredient in this set-up, but a spotlighted instrument.

Suhail was just fourteen when he joined the band, and travelled with them for ten years. His family, however, was very disapproving of this musical phase.

Families, particularly in India, rarely approve of their children taking up a profession in Western pop, rock and allied genres. But Suhail had to face the problem of not only taking to this form of music, but at the same time rejecting a long and established musical tradition of his family. 'My mom threw a fit. Who joins a band? No one. It was unheard of. Now, every Indian classical musician has a band. But if you're from a hereditary Muslim musician's family, you would perform at reputed venues like Kamani or IHC in Delhi. No one goes to a pub called Mez in New Friends Colony, where everyone knows people drink and smoke. I remember coming back from the gig smelling of smoke, and my mom was like, did you smoke? What did you do? What the hell is going on? It was not taken well, to a point where I had to lie when I had rehearsal. I would say I was going for a tuition class, hide my sarangi at my neighbour's house and leave my school bag there. I would come back and say the tuition was great. I had to pay the price of flunking the subject of that tuition class.'

Things began to change on the family front when

Advaita released its first song, 'Hamsadhwani,' in 2003. When Suhail played the track for his grandfather, his doubts that his grandson had been a musical vagabond disappeared. 'My grandfather was all about innovation. Play the instrument as it's supposed to be played – do what you want to, the sky's the limit, that's what being a sarangi player is about.' The etymology of the word sarangi comes from *sau rangi*, the instrument that can evoke 100 colours. Khan Saheb felt that if not one hundred, even a few colours could bring forth the texture and emotivity unique to the sarangi, in whatever context that may be.

During his period with Advaita, Suhail's *talim* slowed down. One decade deep into this phase, he had a moment of reckoning while trying to recall a *bandish* in Yaman that his grandfather had taught him. He had modified his technique to suit his experimental work, but when he tried to play his classical repertoire, he struggled and felt out of touch. 'That was a wake-up call.'

He gradually began extricating himself from the world of collaborative music, though it was difficult and took time. Since he had been active for many years, opportunities came his way and it was difficult to refuse work. He was at a juncture where he considered going to Mumbai to explore working for Bollywood projects, or go West to carve his niche. He chose to go West, going to the UK through various exchange programmes with the British Council. In the UK, he re-explored collaboration through a lens that took him back to his traditional roots. He joined the trio, Yorkston/Thorne/Khan, an acoustic arrangement of guitar, upright bass, and sarangi. Unlike the heavily amplified music he had been playing before, this ensemble explored an approach that showcased the natural sound of the instruments, and the delicate interplay between the different timbres and textures they created when played together.

The band's aesthetic was minimal and folk inspired. Suhail adapted to different roles, sometimes in the lead, sometimes as accompanist, sometimes relating purely on the level of sound. He researched fiddling styles in Scottish songs to inspire different approaches on the sarangi. And while he made an effort to understand the styles he was interacting with, he was conscious to retain the elements of his practice that were important to him. He tuned his instrument in Hindustani classical intervals, sat on the floor rather than on a chair or stool as he had in Advaita, and played acoustic with minimal amplification.

The melodic approach to their work may have been in the realm of raag for Suhail, but he freed himself from that framework when necessary. 'When I'm in these musical outfits, I think of raags as topics, or as a means of language for me to communicate. I'm not thinking of a raag as: this is what it will be. If it's Yaman, yes, I do stick to Yaman initially because that gives me a foundation to build my ideas. That way I know the structure that I will decorate, instead of being stuck at the foundation. But I don't shy away from using notes that are not in Yaman, or sticking only to those classic phrases. I do whatever is required or demanded in that scenario. Awareness of that requirement has come over the years from my lessons on accompaniment and my interactions in Advaita.

'In Yorkston/Thorne/Khan, I've always tried to understand how songs are treated. I think that's something that Hindustani musicians lack. *Bandish*es are songs, but they are being taken for granted. For me, the idea of understanding the song comes from these interactions. I'm trying to think like a song maker, a song writer. Where the song rather than the raag becomes the bigger picture. Where the raag becomes an enhancement of what is happening – it is just one of the wheels of the song. I learned a lot from this experience, and it has enhanced my own execution of *bandish*es and how I structure my classical performances now.'

It seems that the delicate balance of collaboration is knowing when less is more, a moment of restraint. 'Look at the requirements of the song and what it wants from me at this moment. A lot of time it comes down to keeping your ego aside and being honest and just saying no. In Yorkston/Thorne/Khan, there are songs where I'm just playing *sa*, or not playing, or plucking the sarangi strings. If you keep sprinkling it here and there, you've wasted your energy and given all the masala you have. There is only so much masala everyone has.'

Yorkston/Thorne/Khan released three albums in 2016, 2018, and 2020, receiving critical acclaim. The third album was voted as the #1 Folk Album by the *Guardian*, and the band was signed by the reputed London label, Domino Records. While touring the UK, Suhail remembers visiting villages in the countryside filled with completely white British audiences who had no exposure to Indian music or the sarangi. 'It was amazing to educate them and let them know that this is also part of Indian music.'

—

Back in Connecticut, Suhail inhabits a different avatar from the one as a touring, recording musician of Advaita and Yorkston/Thorne/Khan. In a fast turn of events, but perhaps a long-coming transition in his lifetime association with musicians and academics, Suhail found himself applying for PhD programmes in ethnomusicology as his time in the UK was coming to an end. Memories of his childhood with visiting academics and a household filled with books and lively debates circled back into his life. Ethnomusicologist Dan Neuman invited him for a two-week residency at UCLA, where he received his first in-depth exposure to the theorization of musical concepts he had been practising his entire life: *asar*, *riyaz*, *talim*, *taasir*. He was interested in developing his musicality through new avenues. 'I had an intuition that this would not impact my music in a negative way, it could only enhance it. I was also looking forward to it because I was performing so much and not really enjoying it. I wanted a different approach to execution, and I wanted the space and time to work on different material and technique.'

His family, however, was against it. The oft repeated statements amongst musicians surfaced: 'Only people who can't do music do academia.' 'You will lose touch in performance.'

Suhail stuck to his gut and applied, receiving admission at Wesleyan University, a very prestigious ethnomusicology programme that is also known for a strong Carnatic music component (led by T. Viswanathan and by Jon Higgins). He had one week to make his decision. Wesleyan was an interesting choice for Suhail – though it had a rigorous programme, there were no scholars of Hindustani music on the faculty. Located in Middletown, Connecticut, it was quite isolated from urban hubs of performance, like New York or Los Angeles. However, under the close guidance of Dan Neuman, he decided to accept the offer. The lack of a scholar in his area of research would give him freedom to shape his own thought; the geographic isolation would help him focus on his research instead of getting immediately swept into the performance circuit.

Suhail drew upon his lived experiences to guide his research. He used the opportunity to examine the challenges and lack of standardization in sarangi pedagogy, reflecting on the long-held belief that the sarangi is so rarely played because it is simply too difficult. In his opinion, it is not a matter of inherent difficulty, but rather a problem in clarity of thought while teaching.

'The problem with sarangi is that even the teachers have no clarity. It is so mystified, there is no standardization. I'm not saying we need to standardize it, but the concepts are ambiguous. So much so that up until seven years ago, my technique was different from my teachers. I was playing from the upper part of the skin, while my teachers all played from the cuticles. I was struggling for years and wondering, why aren't these ideas coming? I bought time for myself after coming to grad school. I said no to concerts, and I redesigned my technique – from 2016, I started playing from my nail. No one paid attention to what I was doing because they thought it was going fine – *accha, thik hai chal raha hai.* This is also because no one paid attention. That is why it is called such a difficult instrument. Because everything is *uparwale ki marzi.* I also apply cello techniques on the bow, which I teach to my students. There are results, within two weeks you can balance the bow. For intonation, tuning and posture, there are clear exercises. It's just that no one taught these to me. That's the problem. It's not rocket science, it is doable.'

Another important component of his research was recognizing the value of materiality in sarangi playing. 'Materiality was never taught – everything was kept secret, maybe because of competition. This is a hereditary musician telling you this, but nobody told me those things.' This information included where to buy the appropriate bow hair for a desired sound, the kind of wood being used, bridges made of bones, and the process of trying many options to find one that works for each individual's tuning.

The embodied experience of the instrument is also very individualized and often overlooked in training. For Suhail, each person wears their sarangi as customized as they would wear clothes. 'I sometimes copy my uncle who is way bigger than I am – he is 6 feet 3 inches. My grandfather had big hands. I was constantly copying him, unable to execute. It's like I was wearing their oversized clothes, how could I do it? It's only after coming to grad school that I read what other sarangi players have been doing, thanks to research on sarangi players in ethnomusicology. That's my argument in my thesis – to be a sarangi player today, you have to read ethnomusicology. Being a sarangi player is not just limited to technique – it also includes materiality, your own understanding of how you can develop your own sound, which can be enhanced if you read these academically researched books.'

The realities of gaining knowledge of instrument materiality in the world of hereditary musicians is fraught with challenges. Elements of secrecy and loyalty to lineage remain, so much so that the families that possess specialized knowledge of instrument making and sound production will only share this with their sons and nephews. 'I cannot approach these families, I cannot even segue my path to them, because I am a threat. And this won't change. Being a musician is an insecure career.'

Beyond technique, materiality, and pedagogy, the core of Suhail's research is a critical analysis of the Mirasi experience. His childhood memories of Kashipur are inescapable, having seen poverty, discrimination, and lack of social mobility for Mirasis in his community. Though comparatively slightly less than their rural counterparts, Mirasis in urban centres have also faced hierarchy and bias. Historically, Mirasis have been rural village dwellers, largely unmentioned in historical accounts of musical practices and cultures until the 1857 Indian Mutiny. Until this time, records document musicians as Kalavants or Dhadhis (usually referring to vocalists). Mirasis, in contrast, are typically sarangi or tabla artistes, though in the scheme of the musical hierarchy, sarangiyas remain in the bottom rung. In the Mughal courts, artistes were patronized but relegated to their social positions. Private *mehfils* and a culture of music thrived with courtesans and their co-musicians. Under British rule, the local kings and courts upheld a modified system of patronage. However, the Indian Rebellion of 1857 precipitated a sequence of rapid changes for musicians. As the court system faced complete collapse, musicians migrated to urban centres with hopes of better opportunities. Many Mirasis sought opportunities by playing with courtesans, however they faced the colonial stigma and disapproval associated with *tawaif*s. Their status was constantly denigrated.

To adapt to the evolving dynamics of their situation, sarangiyas gave up the instrument and became vocalists, a musical profession accorded more respect and stature. Many of the leading gharanas that are established during this period are a product of vocalists from sarangi lineages.

'They're going to these centres and giving up sarangi because they want more money and don't want discrimination. If you play sarangi, you're not treated well, no one looks at you with a favourable eye. If you came across a sarangi player, a kalavant would say, give up this instrument if you want acceptance in a *mehfil*.

This is because of the way hierarchy has been understood in India – *uttam gaana*, *madhyam bajana*, *nisht nachna*, which is written in *Sangeet Ratnakara*.'

There are written accounts (such as in the book *Sangitagyon Ke Sansmaran* by Ustad Vilayat Hussain Khan) of vocalists describing sarangi players who were trying to become vocalists in *mehfil*s, but were not allowed entry because they were sarangi players. Sarangi players began completely disassociating themselves from that identity to gain acceptance in musical circles. Some of these notable artistes include Ustad Abdul Karim Khan and Ustad Bade Ghulam Ali Khan. Legend has it that Ustad Abdul Karim Khan threw his instrument away because he was so deeply disrespected in court for playing the sarangi.

In his thesis, Suhail introduces the term, 'mirasitude,' inspired by similar movements like 'negritude,' which was coined by French intellectuals to reclaim African culture and consciousness. 'Inspired by them, I came up with the idea of mirasitude, which aims for empowerment from an emic perspective. I wanted to alert scholars about the polysemy and ambiguity attached to this term. The understanding of the term Mirasi as lower caste is wrong. They were identified as low caste because of colonial writings that used the word pejoratively.'

Similarly, Suhail draws the parallel to the colonial view of *tawaif*s. While the British equated *tawaif*s to being sex workers, the reality was that a *tawaif* was a highly specialized expert in multiple fields: music, dance, cuisine, high fashion, shastras, politics and history, often engaging in detailed conversations with intellectual, aristocratic men. They had agency to choose if they wanted to have relations. 'This is a freedom colonial writers couldn't understand. They came from a very Victorian idea of a woman's status and morality. When they witnessed something different in India, they thought, why do women have so much power? They were the ones writing and documenting history from their own point of view and understanding, imposing laws and values from their ideas of right and wrong. That becomes the foundation of our nationalism and efforts to naturalize, purify and sacralize music. We know what danger it has given us.'

The Mirasi plight is layered – on one hand it is stoked by the internal community-based bias and desire for disassociation, and on the other, the colonial narrative that permeated texts and elite culture and instilled long lasting stigma.

'My hope is that Mirasis themselves, in the future, will start using this term with a feeling of empowerment rather than just disassociating from it. I'm well aware of the pain, discrimination and oppressed lifestyles that have gone behind it. I want us to move beyond that and look forward. Also, I want to raise awareness about the amazing things Mirasis have done for Hindustani music in the twentieth and twenty-first century for the music to evolve. This dissertation is very unique – the first time one has been written from the point of view of a hereditary sarangi player.'

One contribution of the community that goes largely unrecognized is the way in which Mirasi musicians converted theoretical knowledge to practical application. Suhail shares the legend of Dhadhi-dhrupadiya, Behram Khan, who disguised himself as a Brahmin to learn the theoretical scholarship from the Brahmin scholars of the period. He converted this knowledge into practice and began teaching it to Mirasis – one such area being mastery of Merukhand technique.

Suhail is very self-aware that the academic space affords him the security and support to speak about an issue that is both sensitive and personal to him. 'I am very comfortable coining the term mirasitude because it benefits me, makes me look good in America. I don't know how people in India will feel when I go back. I worry about it. I worry about what my relatives and peers will feel when they read about mirasitude.'

In contemporary times, it is impossible to talk about Indian music without referring to the social conditions that surround its practice. T.M. Krishna, for example, has spotlighted many of the contradictions of caste bias that have afflicted Carnatic music. In the world of Hindustani music, however, dialogue and discourse around issues of caste and religion are yet to enter the mainstream. Despite the art form's syncretic history, the ecosystem does not necessarily embrace or uplift the diversity of its practitioners. Suhail's experience as a hereditary Muslim musician brings to light the presence of caste bias internal to Muslim society in India, as well as external biases from the general music community.

The question of Islam and music is one that Suhail wrestles with through a life that has seen orthodox belief, spirituality, and a form of Islam that he calls 'Indianized Islam.' One of his earliest memories from Kashipur captures the complexity of this paradox – a memory that contains the unexpected beauty of his inherited tradition along with the pain of his identity in a small town.

Though he went through the rigmarole of *talim* with his grandfather and uncle, Suhail received many unofficial lessons from the women in his household, who were silent repositories of knowledge that often went undocumented. During the period of Muharram, a month celebrating the New Year of Islam as well as a period mourning the martyrdom of the Prophet's grandson, Suhail's family was immersed in the tradition of singing *marsiya*s, elegiac songs that tell the story of the battle between the Prophet's grandson (Hussayn Ibn Ali) and Yazid I. Interestingly, they are all composed in raags, and narrate the story of the battle while highlighting acts of heroism.

'My training of raag Shahana was completely through *marsiya*s. I also heard raags like Gauri, Lalita Gauri, and Deshkar this way. Though men also sing *marsiya*s, it has largely been archived and carried on by women. My paternal grandmother knew hundreds of *marsiya*s.'

Within the house, music may have been spontaneous and free-flowing, but outside, all attachment to music had to be stifled. 'On one hand, when you leave the house, you don't even want to be called a musician, let alone a Mirasi. Inside the house, you're singing laurels, telling stories about performances. During Muharram, you're playing dhol-tashe and singing *marsiyas*. It was so full of music. I was literally losing my head. I was going through an identity crisis. Kashipur was too much for me, way too much. Inside the house there was so much music, outside the house, you zip it up. You transform yourself into something else, because you want acceptance from society.'

Despite the fact that Muslim women in hereditary music families were largely relegated to a domestic role – not being allowed to learn or perform music like the men or boys in the family – they played a critical part in shaping the next generation's rising stars. 'Women play a very important role in choosing who will become the torchbearer. They observe and see who will put in hard work and come up. While Ustads are busy concertizing, women are so attuned to the kids. They know, *kis me oomph hai, kis me charisma hai.* They work like a clan together. They have a very in-depth knowledge of music as feeling, not just technique or skill. Often when I was practising, my mom used to come and tell me, "You sound like a cat dying." Though she wouldn't give me feedback on how not to sound, because she didn't know herself, she had been surrounded by incredible music, and she had the reference of *bandishes*. And the same applies to other women in my family as well, her sisters, my mom's aunties – they were very sharp and knowledgeable.'

Roshanara Begum stands apart as the only popularly known female Mirasi musician from a golden era of musicians. Unlike others who may have had the talent, she had support from her husband, a man who recognized her ability, supported her singing, and believed that her music should be heard. 'Now, a lot of musicians in my family are teaching music to their daughters, because they've also realized that it's hard to live a life with no job or skill. Perceptions are changing, which is good,' Suhail reflects.

In his larger family, he observed his own relatives evolve on a scale of orthodoxy, balancing religion with their beliefs about music. Many became more observant later in their life, a trend that Suhail sees as a very Indianized Islam, as opposed to the largely prevalent Wahabi Islamic culture that has set a global tone for the religion. Indianized Islam allows for a more fluid and evolving relationship with religion, incorporating elements of local language and culture. The notion of deepening religious practice at a later age could also be construed as quintessentially Indian – religious practice surfaces after other responsibilities in life have been completed.

When it comes to the Indianized culture of Islam in Hindustani music, there are countless examples. In his own family, when his grandfather came home for the first time after marriage, his mother performed an aarti in front of him before he entered the house. Similarly, many musicians would finish their namaz, immediately followed by *riyaz* of *bandish*es that could be in praise of Hindu gods. Such juxtapositions were so common and normal.

Though it is comforting to believe that such practices stem from notions of oneness and pan-religiosity, Suhail considers the fact that these could have emerged as adaptive strategies over shifting historical powers. 'When you trace any Muslim family in India back five to six generations, they were all Hindus. Maybe they accepted Islam because they thought it was a better way of life, a more civilized way of human living that gave greater social mobility. Maybe it was because of the ruling power at the time. Lot of times, musicians were saying and doing things, practising values, in relation to what was needed and what people wanted to see. Everyone is trying to look for acceptance in Indian society, to claim authenticity, to claim purity. That's happening in all stratas.'

In this Indianized Islam, Suhail observed people in his family who practiced, people who believed *riyaz* was an approach to God, some who read the Quran every day, some who smoked cigarettes and drank alcohol. Suhail does not believe that Islamic texts imply that music is *haram*, though that has been a widespread belief among many subsects of Islam. In Sufism, he finds tolerance, a core Islamic value that has been lost in translation. Here, the message of Islam spreads through the medium of music, a process in which Mirasis have played a very important role. Many Mirasis, who are sarangiyas and tabaliyas, have found their spiritual path through Sufism, particularly the Chishtiya order of Sufism that embraces music.

After the loss of his grandfather, Suhail experienced a spiritual vacuum. Being out of India and away from the atmosphere in which his spirituality was woven into the fabric of day-to-day life, Suahil felt lost. He found anchoring in Iyengar yoga, a practice that reminded him of his musical training in its specificity and rigour of movement.

For Suhail, spirituality – in whatever blended shape that may take – cannot be separated from the practice of music. 'This music cannot be worked without having some sort of centrality to yourself, and that comes from spirituality. We really need to have clarity in our thoughts to be able to execute these phrases, they should make sense. Phrasing sentences, clarity, calmness, holding yourself, confidence, ownership, and authority all come when you are aligned. That is my understanding and what I think being spiritual is.'

What does it mean to be a Mirasi hereditary musician in 2024?

In comparison to its history of syncretic traditions and practitioners, the contemporary landscape of Hindustani music is dominated by musicians from a more homogenized background. The demographics indicate performers who are middle and upper middle-class Hindus. Suhail acknowledges feelings of fear, insecurity, and exclusion amongst hereditary communities. 'When we look at nationalizing, claims of identity and authority, theorizing ideas, who does it benefit? It has to benefit someone, and simultaneously snatch something from someone? That's how these things work. We are left in a massive mess.'

In addition to the obstacles hereditary musicians faced in smaller towns and cities, the current trend in big cities and festivals involves a heavy online and social media presence, dictated by algorithms and paid promotion, complicating the formula for visibility further. 'Now you're giving a platform for someone who couldn't have imagined themselves sitting on a stage twenty or thirty years ago. Hats off to that. But don't exclude someone who's spent generations on the art form and is carrying something with a very different kind of an impact.'

Suhail reflects on the label and associated responsibility of being a hereditary musician in the current scenario. 'We musicians are storytellers, hereditary or not. Hereditary musicians specially grew up with more stories in their bank. Those stories carry music. So go back and dig into those stories and make sense of them and apply them to your music. That's what it means to be a hereditary musician.'

He is trying to explore the balance between responsibility and freedom, agency amidst suppression and discrimination. The notion of responsibility is not only towards the music and its preservation, but also for the support and upliftment of the community. And in examining these paradigms, he also questions the need to identify with this label to begin with. 'Is it authenticating my own musicality when I say I'm a hereditary musician, does it make me better, or different?' Asking the question seems more important than coming to an answer.

On a crisp and chilly November night in Brooklyn, I had another opportunity to perform with Suhail at a venue that serves eclectic health food and provides a psychedelic space for performance, yoga, and wellness. We share a knowing laugh about how hipster vibes somehow meet Hindustani music in the modern age.

I begin with the raag Shyam Kalyan, '*Mhara rasiya, balma*,' a composition that oozes with the pining of one lover for another. A pining so deep that is not limited to just one, but several lifetimes. As we perform together, I realize that only the sarangi can evoke the complex shades of emotions that reside on the spectrum of love and separation: its sound single handedly encompasses both beauty and pain. Are they not two sides of the same coin? After Shyam Kalyan, I sing raag Shahana, a raag Suhail learned from the *marsiya*s of his paternal grandmother, and one that I have absorbed in the classic guru-shishya format. I reflect on how vastly different our musical memories of this raag must be, and yet how seamlessly we are able to converse in its language. Our musical interplay forms a painting that draws upon a wide palette of experience, culture, and history. A painting that tells a story of musical inheritance, discovery, and hope for change.

8

SHUBHA JOSHI

Voicing the Feminine

THE MODERN CONCERT FORMAT IN HINDUSTANI VOCAL music has become formulaic. In a typical performance of ninety minutes, *khayal* reigns as king for the majority of the concert, and for some relief and contrast, the last few minutes are reserved for the 'lighter' forms such as *thumri, dadra*, or *kajri*. I often wonder what is meant by this notorious term, *light*? Is it light because of its short duration? Is it light because of the theme of its lyrics? Is it light because of the treatment and ornamentation of the notes? Is it light because of the limited range of raags typically featured in these forms? Is it light because of the supposed absence of a shastra-based approach? Whatever the rationalization, it neither seems to be an appropriate or accurate label, because mastery of these forms requires specialized training and just as much effort as *khayal* or its allied genres.

These questions raised more doubts for me. Do musical

forms get hierarchized? Just as hierarchies are constructed in society, is there a similar hierarchy of styles and forms of Hindustani music? The dominance of shastric culture in Hindustani music has made *khayal* practitioners the face of this musical form. It is rare to find specialized or exclusive practitioners of *thumri* in the contemporary music landscape. But if there is one person whose lifetime efforts answered the questions I was grappling with, it was Shubha Joshi.

Standing outside what I believed to be Shubhaji's flat, I peek in through the grill on the top half of a classic Mumbai-style door. Through the narrow slots, a stunning picture of Shobha Gurtu catches my eye as the wobbly sound of an electronic tanpura cuts through the thick monsoon air. I know I've reached the right place, and Shubhaji slowly comes to the door to let me in. The aura of musical endeavour is palpable – the walls are filled with photographs of Ustads and younger pictures of Shubhaji that remind one of a vintage era of LPs, alongside numerous certificates and awards. It was as though I time travelled into a musical world that no longer existed.

Shobha Gurtu, whose portrait I had just spotted on the wall, is known the world over for a certain quality that only few vocalists possess: a voice exuding expression and a musical temperament steeped in emotion. It was perhaps the only way she knew to be, to feel deeply and use music as her ultimate vehicle of expression. Her voice was a container of contradictory qualities: syrupy yet textured, grainy yet velvety, tonally rich yet light with agility. Perhaps because of her larger-than-life persona and stage presence, the fact that she trained several exceptional musicians in their own right, some of whom take her repertoire and style forward, is less known. Shubha Joshi is one of them.

Shubhaji's voice has a similarly alluring old world quality, thick and deep in tone. But beyond the voice – which is to a certain extent a physiological and genetic phenomenon – it is musicianship that carries the gift of the voice beyond the realm of anatomy and into artistic expression. Shubhaji's life has been devoted to crafting this musicianship, and it has been done quietly, consistently, and obstinately.

Shubhaji's calling to study and sing these forms was undeniable and nothing could stop her pursuit. The path that led her there was not linear, filled with rigorous musical foundations, personal sacrifice, and a long roster of colourful personalities comprised of gurus and musical colleagues.

Born in Ujjain to Kusum and Dr Narayan Vishnu Joshi, Shubhaji was one of four children. Her father had a doctorate in literature and was a professor of philosophy from Banaras Hindu University. A master of many languages, including Russian, German, French, he also published some of his own work in philosophy. In Varanasi, where music was often heard on the riverbanks and the ghats, the *mahaul* was conducive for learning. Dr Joshi began lessons in vocal music alongside his studies, and after moving to Mumbai, he eventually became head of the philosophy department at Ruia College and lived in the vibrant musical hub of Borivali.

Although she belonged to a music loving family, Shubhaji did not come from a lineage of musicians. Her father bought a gramophone player that filled their home with the sounds of Bismillah Khan, Bade Ghulam Ali Khan, Abdul Karim Khan, Faiyaz Khan, and Kesarbai Kerkar. Among the classical singers, Shubhaji only liked the sweet voice of Abdul Karim Khan and her heart was always drawn to the music of Lata Mangeshkar and Asha Bhosle. She would often be caught humming and copying her favourite film songs or Marathi *bhavgeet*, lost in the headiness of her own musical bubble. Shubhaji's mother also had an aptitude for music, completing her matriculation in music. Though Shubhaji would listen to her *riyaz* and imitate whatever she was singing, she never learned from her. Classical music was not her initial calling.

The world of film music was enticing, popular, glamorous, and instantly appealing. But the more she copied this style of music, the more conscious she became of the quality of her voice. 'When I realized that Lataji sings on such a high pitch, I was so sad. I couldn't sing on that *sur*. I have a very heavy voice, *kali teen ki aavaaz* (F# on the harmonium). Though I sang well, people around and near me were used to hearing these songs in Lataji's voice. I was so disappointed and saddened by this. Though I was happy with my music, my voice was rejected in so many places, like auditions and school programmes.'

Despite this, Shubhaji's father noticed her innate

talent and channelled it into music lessons. He sent her to Master Pandurang Amberkar, a musician of the Bhendi Bazar gharana and disciple of gharana maestro Ustad Aman Ali Khan. When her father had first heard Aman Ali Khan Saheb live in concert, he was so impressed that he wanted to learn from him as soon as possible. He was directed to his closest source and shishya, Amberkar Master. He would begin lessons with Masterji, and eventually introduce his wife and daughters to him for lessons as well.

—

Shubhaji and her younger sister started training with Amberkar Master when she was eleven years old. Every Saturday after a half day of school in Vile Parle, the sisters would meet their mother at the train station to travel to Grant Road for class with Masterji, returning back to their home in Kandivali at the end of the long day.

Masterji's approach to teaching classical music was not the typical format that would be expected. He believed in peaking the student's curiosity and interest before flooding her with exercises and rote learning. Rather than starting with note exercises and scales like *alankar*s and *palta*s, he began by teaching small *bandish*es, many that were already popular from films. For instance, Shubhaji first learned raag Malkauns from the famous film composition, '*Man Tarpat Hari Darshan Ko*' from the film *Baiju Bawra*. Similarly, he would teach them appealing *bhajan*s that made singing fun, rather than drudgery they were forced to do. Gradually, he would transition into more traditional repertoire, but by this time, students did not need to be convinced or coaxed into learning classical music; they were sold.

Masterji would play the tabla himself as he taught the children. While teaching them *bandish*es, he would repeatedly bring their attention to the main markers of the taal, insisting they give taal by hand as they sang small fixed variations and pre-composed *taan*s. Masterji's approach was to initially expose students to all musical elements without excessive analysis or definition. Musical ornaments – such as *meend*, *khatka*, *kan*, or *murki* – would be embedded in the repertoire. These were introduced without simplification right from the beginning, and these nuances sat in the voices of young children without their knowing the nomenclature. It was more important that they could execute these flourishes than be able to label them. The goal was to imprint an accurate and aesthetic sound memory in their mind.

'Sing the notes with love. You're not throwing stones!' he would say to them.

Though their class was only once a week, (Masterji taught music in a school during the week), Shubhaji managed to gain a foundation in a variety of raags as well as a grip over *sur ka tehraav* (the steadiness and stability of a note), and *madhya laya* taal *mei tehraav* (holding the pace of a medium tempo composition). However, during these classes with her sister, Shubhaji was subconsciously aware of how her quality of voice did not conform to societal expectations. 'My sister's voice was thin and nice. Masterji would often tell my mother, "She (my sister) is my shehnai, and the other one is okay." This made me very sad. At that time, I felt like there was something lacking in me, but I realized later on that my voice was unique.'

Interestingly, it was only when Shubhaji auditioned for a seat at SNDT University, Mumbai, that the concepts of gharana and *gayaki* were first brought to her attention. After an impressive audition for the music department, the auditioner asked her which gharana she was trained in. She had never heard the word gharana before, so she innocently and honestly told the examiner that she had learned from Amberkar Masterji, and that is all she knew on the matter. When she met her guru next, she asked him, 'What is this thing that they call gharana?' He had a hearty laugh and explained that the gharana she had been trained in is known as the 'Bhendi Bazaar gharana,' founded by Chhajju Khan Saheb, and taken forward by his son Aman Ali Khan.

'Bhendi Bazaar *kaisa naam hai* (What kind of a name is Bhendi Bazaar)?' Shubhaji asked, after learning that the other gharanas had more stately names like Gwalior, Agra, and Jaipur. Masterji proceeded to tell her the story of a family lineage of musicians that included businessmen, such as Aman Ali Khan Saheb's uncle. Bhendi Bazaar, which is located in southern Mumbai, is a name that went through a sort of bastardization. During the colonial period, the Britishers loosely referred to the area as 'Behind the Bazaar,' after which the local residents unwittingly adapted it to 'Bhendi Bazaar.' The name stuck, not only for the bazar, but for the gharana as well.

As Masterji enumerated the features of this *gayaki*, Shubhaji realized that she had been imbibing it unknowingly over the years in her *talim*. 'The prominent feature of our *gayaki* is the focus on note-by-note development, gradually going from one to the next one, creating many varieties of permutations and combinations in the *merukhand* style (a pyramid pattern of notes that explores all arrangements of a given set of notes). While doing *alap* within the *khayal*, we use the words. This was compulsory for us, we were not allowed to sing only in *aakar*. Masterji would say, "Use the words and sing, or else what are the words of *bandish* there for? Then the *bhav* will naturally follow on its own." It is all about poetry, notes and their ornamentation, and how they all come together. These are features of the style. Masterji had taught us that this is a very peaceful style of singing in which partaking in the joy of *sur* is the priority.'

Purity of textual diction was also an important tenet. It is believed that Aman Ali Khan Saheb would often say, '*Shuddh bani, shuddh mudra*,' referring not only to accurate pronunciation (unaffected by regional accents), but also to maintaining undistorted facial gestures while singing. In an effort to create a style that stood apart from the other gharanas, Aman Ali Khan travelled to South India and learned elements of Carnatic music – the style of *sargam*, in particular, was something that he enjoyed and chose to incorporate into his own music. These features amalgamated to form an identity for this relatively young gharana, compared to the others that had a longer generational history.

Shubhaji continued to learn from Masterji until her college years at SNDT, and as she advanced in her music he asked her to also train under his guru bhais and senior musicians, Ramesh Nadkarni and Master Navrang. For her college exams, she had to master forms such as *dhrupad* and *dhamar*, in addition to *khayal*. When given the choice to study other forms including *natyageet*, *thumri*, *dadra*, she was certain that she would choose *thumri* and *dadra*. She did not enjoy *natyageet*. As she said, 'It only featured a highly prepared and practiced voice, fast *taan*s, and the aesthetics of the language felt very aggressive to me.' She opted for *thumri* and *dadra*, and perhaps at this pivotal moment in her musical trajectory, she had the opportunity to witness a concert that changed her path forward.

The music department at SNDT organized a concert by Shobha Gurtu, and for the first time in her life, Shubhaji heard a voice that sounded like hers. 'A light bulb lit in my head, a lamp was lit ablaze. I was so thrilled that this kind of voice could produce such beautiful music. I was determined that I will learn and sing this type of music.' Still, as she was finishing her BA, she was unable to go to Shobhaji, and relied on the collection in the university library to learn the repertoire needed for her exams. She would park herself in the library, put on the designated headphones, and listen and re-listen until she imprinted the iconic recordings in her mind. 'After repeated listening, I by hearted Girija Devi's *thumri*, "*Itni araj mori.*" I memorized it without thinking and sang it for the exam. I graduated with a gold medal and first rank in the entire university. It was because of Masterji that I could learn so much.'

Shubhaji received a national scholarship to pursue her MA. At this point, she became much more fixated on the idea of learning from Shobha Gurtu and approached her through one of the faculty at her college. Right from their first meeting, Shubhaji saw the unfiltered and unusually honest demeanour of this musical legend. As she reclined on her couch and listened to the young Shubha sing a *ghazal*, Shobhaji was so taken by the composition that she immediately said, 'Teach this to me too!' It was not a casual statement made in passing, or a moment of inspired praise. Moments after Shubha finished singing, Shobhaji insisted that she write down the lyrics for her. Shobha Gurtu was an artiste without any airs and a thirst to sing anything that touched her heart. Whenever she recognized beautiful music (no matter who it was coming from), she would not miss the opportunity to learn it and make it her own.

When Shubhaji told her father that she wanted to learn *thumri* from Shobha Gurtu, she faced significant resistance. He firmly put his foot down against it, insisting that she stick to her classical roots. If she really felt so inclined, he suggested that she could sing classical compositions in *deepchandi*, the taal in which *thumris* were typically sung. After all, *thumris* were sung by *kothevalis*, or courtesans. You won't be able to sing it, you should stick to classical music, he told her.

By this stage in her personal life, Shubhaji had made it very clear that she did not want to get married; her life would be devoted to the pursuit of music, and she did not have the time or interest in marriage. Though she faced family pressure to get married and hold a more conventional job, Shubhaji held her ground. 'I have chosen this path and I don't want to disturb its trajectory. I don't want to do a regular job either, because if I do, the whole day will be lost, and then when will I get the time to learn and do *riyaz*? If I am to do this music in full seriousness, for which you need almost a full day to practise, how will I do it? If I had taken a bank job, my music would have gone. I am very stubborn, so nobody could change my mind.'

This decision would come up again during her initial tussles to learn from Shobha Gurtu, when her father questioned how an unmarried woman like her could capture the amorous sentiment of a *thumri*. Her father told her, 'If you don't want to get married, how do you expect to sing *thumri*? You don't have the disposition to sing *thumri*, *sringar* music.' Shubhaji had a quick answer for her father. 'Tell me, how many married women sing *thumris* well? I take it as a challenge to sing and prove you wrong. After that, he remained quiet on the matter. I don't agree with this way of thinking – *sringar bhav* needs to be in your mind, and everyone has the capacity to feel that. If it is there in your mind, then you can bring it into your singing. Just because you don't get married doesn't mean that you are a *saadhvi*. I began going to Shobhaji, and he never asked me again.'

Once a week, Shubhaji made her trip to Grant Road, where Shobhaji lived. Initially, she assumed that her strong classical foundations would make it easy to pick up *thumri – how tough could it be?* 'Only when I began going for lessons did I realize that this is very hard. However much classical training you have, this is not that easy.' It soon became evident that weekly classes were insufficient to pick up the ocean of nuances and compositions that Shobhaji had to offer. By the end of her train ride back home to Kandivali, she struggled to remember all that had happened in the class. It was the 1970s, and there was no way to record classes back then – Shubhaji became very nervous about how she would learn in this fashion. Four months into their sessions, she asked Shobhaji if she could attend other students' classes. She agreed, and Shubhaji began attending classes every day, often sitting in the class of another senior student, Sarla Bhide.

Learning from Shobha Gurtu was not your typical music lesson. As an uncontainable creative spirit, each class was shaped by her mood and state of mind. And the concert stage was just as much a classroom as the home, if not more. Students had to watch her every move – from her selection of repertoire, her stage presence, her relationship with her co-artistes, and her deep involvement with the music – and apply it to their music. Very close observation and imitation were critical skills in absorbing her style. As a guru, her method of teaching was like a dialogue of exchange, exuding a way of being that was infectious to all around her.

During *talim*, Shobhaji would teach both her iconic and lesser-known repertoire (including rare *bandish*es), ensuring the finer and subtler points of pronunciation were not overlooked. The nodes of nasality in the word '*saanvariyaan*,' for instance. Students had to copy her in every way – the throw of her voice, the inflections of her diction, the variety of embellishments, or *harkat*s, she would produce in her voice. Each genre had to be understood for its own aesthetic sensibilities, and the same approach could not be applied from *thumri* to *ghazal* or *bhajan*. The presence of these subtleties is not limited to the composition – their presence is felt even in the treatment of the opening *alap* to the composition. An opening *alap* for a *thumri* should not sound like an *alap* for a *bandish*, Shubhaji pointed out. There should be differences in the way the voice is thrown (*avaaz ka lagao*), the ornaments of the phrases, and their pacing. Similarly, within the composition, the development style of a *dadra* would be akin to the treatment of a *chhota khayal*, and a slow *thumri* would be like a *vilambit*. *Alap*s in a *chhota khayal* are shorter in length and faster in pace, and in a *vilambit khayal*, they are longer and slightly slower in pace. In a *dadra*, a cycle of six beats that is usually fast paced, the development would move at an even faster pace, in which the words are almost spoken in musical cadence.

Command over numerous languages and dialects is an essential effort to retain a flavour of authenticity and aesthetic cohesiveness. *Thumri* and *dadra* compositions primarily use Brij Bhasha and Avadhi, but just as the voice has a certain throw, so do words. For this particular quality of *ucchar* and *kahan*, Shubhaji follows the Benares *thumri* singers – Siddheshwari Devi, Rasoolan Bai, Hira Devi Mishra, and Girija Devi. 'These musicians are from that region – the throw of the language comes naturally from the spoken language. That must be copied. We are from Maharashtra, so we must pay close attention to their approach, *bhasha ka abhyaas* (practise of language).'

Shubhaji practices what she preaches, especially when it comes to *ghazal*s. 'If you're going to sing *ghazal*s, you must know Urdu,' Shubhaji says as she proudly shows me the certificate she received after three and a half years of Urdu training in which she mastered conversation, *ucchar* (accent), reading, and writing.

Her serious efforts paid off. During an All India Radio audition, she presented some of the *ghazal*s she learned from Shobhaji. One of the judges was the famous Urdu poet, Majrooh Sultanpuri, and the other was the renowned music director duo Shankar–Jaikishan. Though the auditions were blind, the judges broke protocol and called Shubhaji inside after she sang. They wanted to tell her in person that they were so impressed with her singing that they gave her a 'direct A grade' – a rare occurrence in a system that makes musicians apply for gradual upgradation over many years. This fateful audition led to 'chain booking' concerts in AIR stations in multiple cities: Mumbai, Aurangabad, Jaipur, and Udaipur.

In Aurangabad, one station director gave Shubhaji a bit of a scare when he mentioned a laundry list of *ghazals* that she should include in her repertoire. She went back to Mumbai and requested Shobhaji to compose more *ghazal*s that she could perform, but Shobhaji told her that many of the *ghazal*s she sang were composed by Taj Ahmed Khan. If she wanted to learn more in this genre, she would have to go to him.

In the meanwhile, Shubhaji gained tremendous experience and confidence by performing extensively with Shobhaji. Shobhaji pushed her on stage, insisting that she accompany her on tanpura and vocal support during most concerts – this experience helped her face her fear of performance and insecurities about her voice. 'Her performances, *that* is where we had to learn. At home, sometimes she would sing in full mood and there too, we had to listen very closely. The truth was she didn't want to teach. She was not a teacher. She was a performer. It is rare that a performer is also a good teacher.'

While providing vocal support, Shubhaji learned under pressure in the public eye. These learnings were perhaps the most impactful. It was a feat to match and perfect Shobhaji's *sur* and throw of voice. It was equally demanding to follow Shobhaji's tremendous rhythmic mastery – the *mukhda* could emerge seamlessly from any point of the taal cycle with utmost grace and aesthetics. Shobhaji was equally at ease adapting a composition into any taal or *laya* on stage, based on the capability of her tabla player. At the performative level, students would observe Shobhaji's gestures and facial expressions, drawn from her childhood training in dance. Shobhaji embodied performance in totality – this way of being could not be taught, but internalized through close and frequent association. 'In front of the audience, Shobhaji would just sparkle. Her voice was top class. I had the opportunity to learn and listen to so much. So many times, I had tears in my eyes listening to her – even she would have tears in her eyes while singing.'

Beyond the musical nitty-gritty, there was much to learn by studying the precise manner in which Shobhaji could gauge the pulse of the audience and have them spellbound within moments. 'She knew which things the audience would respond to, what they wanted. How much to give, what balance of classical and *thumri* – observing these selections was just as important as looking at how she presented her music,' Shubhaji recalls.

Mimesis, or imitative learning, is a very common method used in Hindustani music for the initial portion of training. In this phase, the act of doing is more important than knowing the 'why' behind the doing. It is a phase of skill building, knowledge assimilation, voice culturing, and honing of listening. Through keen observation and imitation, Shubhaji assimilated much of the unteachable. With increased visibility and association with Shobhaji, she started to receive concert invitations for her solo performances. Naturally, organizers wanted to hear Shobhaji's repertoire, and she received numerous requests. It was an opportunity for Shubhaji to assess her ability in this art form, to see where she had reached as an independent musician and thinker. During this period of performance, one criticism she received made her question the value of copying her guru. 'One organizer told me, "Your classical music is very nice, but it seems like you sing *thumri* just like Shobhaji. How long will you continue copying her? What is yours in that rendition?"'

After hearing this comment, she felt compelled to parse out its validity. She asked Shobhaji what she thought of this feedback, and remembers very vividly. 'But you have to copy! I copied her response Begum Akhtar. Those artistes that we idealize, whose music we like, we must copy them, isn't it? In the beginning you have to copy, and later on, after repeated singing, you make it your own,' Shobhaji said.

Outside of their musical interactions, Shubhaji got glimpses into an innocent and free-spirited side of Shobhaji. At times, she would tag along to Shobhaji's mother's (Menaka bai) house, with whom Shobhaji had a rather fraught relationship. Menaka bai did not want Shobhaji to get married, and this tension seemed to ebb and flow in their dynamic. To appease her, Shobhaji would take Shubhaji along to her mother's house to cheer her up. They would pass time by having golgappas or watching movies together. Shobhaji was also a skilled and enthusiastic cook. Shubhaji remembers when she visited her family's home in Kandivali after a concert and spent the night. The next day, she woke up and insisted on cooking for the entire family, making her special alu matar that required Shubhaji to grind a special masala by hand in the mortar and pestle. 'I got so fed up grinding that paste, but she kept insisting it had to be finer and finer! Even today everyone in my family remembers that taste – Shobhaji's rasa bhaji.'

After Shubhaji finished her BA in music, her father retired from his position as a professor. The family had managed within limited financial means – her father received a modest salary to support a family of six. When he retired, he told Shubhaji that she had to take care of her own expenses. She received a ₹100 scholarship for her MA, and her brother, who was in America, sent her extra money to supplement her costs. After this, she began teaching music privately, but to support herself completely as a freelance musician in Mumbai was no easy task. Much of her earnings came from radio and recording work.

She recalls the challenges she encountered and her adaptive strategies. 'My voice was heavy, so I didn't get as much work. But by staying in the film industry, do you know what I learned? In choral projects, there was a need for voices like Lataji's, so I managed to sing like that using a falsetto, not the voice I used in *mehfil*s. I learned to change the track of my voice as needed, and this is how I earned money.'

She was selected for the Akashvani choir, and that was her first taste of a lucrative job. She earned ₹500 per month, singing patriotic choral songs in many different languages, often arranged with harmonies. It was an opportunity to apply her vocal skills in a different context and learn new techniques. 'Though it was very tough to remember the harmonies, we really enjoyed it, and I remember those songs even now. Because my voice was different, the music director, Kanu Ghosh, gave me the opportunity to lead many solos. Choir singing is another style of singing all together.'

They were coached by experts to sing in many different languages – Bengali, Odia, Assamese, Sindhi, Gujarati, Kacchi, Konkani, Marathi, Hindi, Tamil, and Kannada. In this way, she increased her exposure to languages and many varieties of songs including the folk genre. Every month they learned a new song, first grasping the outline of the composition, then working on the diction, and finally putting together the layers of harmony. She enjoyed working there for five years, until the programme was stopped.

While training with Shobhaji, she found herself getting more solo recording opportunities. Her very first solo recording was for a weekly radio programme called *Amruthavani* that featured *bhajans*. In addition to learning from Shobhaji, she also studied under well-known singer and composer Ninu Majumdar and *thumri* exponent Kaumudi Munshi. Her association with them came through her friendship with their daughter and her college classmate, Rajul Mehta. Shubhaji learned new and rare repertoire from all members of the family. 'Ninu Majumdar really liked my voice. He also taught me *thumri* and *dadra*, and Kaumudi Munshi was a disciple of Siddheshwari Devi. I would keep dropping in and out of their house. Ninu bhai composed and taught me the *bhajan* for my first recording, a Marwadi *bhajan*, "*Bharmayo Mharo, Mharo Do.*" That was my first experience in the studio, singing with headphones. I found it very difficult, because we are used to keeping the tanpura close to our ears. In the beginning, they asked me why I was not singing. I couldn't hear the tanpura or the rhythm track. Then, I took off the headphones and sang with the sound from the speakers.'

With time, she became an expert at studio technique, and was called by legendary music directors Jaidev and Jagjit. She was considered for films that featured music leaning towards *thumri*, *dadra*, and those that fell into the *mujra* category. *Mujra* is a style of music that was performed in the courts and *kotha*s, combining the styles of *thumri* and *dadra* with a leaning towards kathak. In those days, musicians were called to the director's home to learn the music and rehearse before going into the studio. Because of her extensive training, she was able to pivot easily between genres, keeping the stylistic differences and vocal technique separate. Her ability to pick up melodies very quickly with aesthetic precision came in very useful in the studio setting. Her favourite work in film was for the popular film *Sardari Begum*, directed by Shyam Benegal, with music composed by Vanraj Bhatia. The film tells the story of a *thumri* singer who dies in a Hindu–Muslim riot. In the popular song, '*Sanwariya Dekh Zara*,' it is evident that Shubhaji thrives in the genre she has specialized in over the years.

Because of the popularity of dance in Indian film, many songs were akin to *mujra*s, or a mix of *mujra*s and *dadra*s. 'Whatever I sang, I sang with honesty, from my heart and mind. I didn't like *mujra*s very much, because sometimes the words are a bit vulgar. I couldn't accept that. There were a few times I refused to sing such songs. The lyricists would also be present, so sometimes I would request them to change the words. Artistes new to the field don't say anything, they worry that people will think less of them or that they will lose opportunities and it will go to someone else. I didn't think like that. If I don't get it, then let it be. I wouldn't sing songs below my dignity.'

She discovered that the greatest challenge of getting drawn into a career of recording was the amount of time it took away from her *riyaz*. 'It was so difficult. I had put in so much effort in music, and I knew that all the greats put in long hours of *riyaz*. I couldn't even do two. If I did proper *riyaz* in the morning and evening for four days, I would be so happy. And on the fifth day, I would have to go to the studio for a recording. If *riyaz* didn't happen, I would be very troubled.'

—

'Half of my life has gone into learning,' Shubhaji says, while giving me chai and poha.

The itch to learn *ghazal* in its most authentic form was strong, and Shubhaji followed Shobhaji's advice to seek tutelage under the renowned *ghazal* composer and musician, Taj Ahmed Khan. She went to his home in Mahim to ask if he would accept her as a student. Though he agreed, he gave her the run around for six to seven months before he would actually begin teaching her. 'He avoided me for a long time. He said there were issues with his health. Or that he didn't have time, and I should come after one month. I was absolutely determined that he was the only person I could study *ghazal* with, though other musicians were available in Mumbai. I was drawn to his style in particular.' Finally, Shubhaji put it to him as bluntly as possible: 'Tell me properly, will you teach me? I don't like travelling up and down every time like this.'

After this, he took immediate action and conducted the *ganda bandhan* ceremony, commemorating the occasion with a composition in Mishra Megh. Though he used to travel and teach most of his students in their own homes, Shubhaji was asked to come to his house, and she was very grateful to have this privilege. 'To learn *thumri* and *ghazal*, it is very necessary to be in that *mahaul* (atmosphere), to hear the language, and be part of the culture.'

Learning from Khan Saheb demanded a great deal of patience on the part of the student. 'He would call me home at 11 a.m., but when I would get there, he would still be lying in bed. He would slowly get up, ask his wife for chai in bed. After two or three more servings of chai, he would go to the bathroom, brush his teeth, then have breakfast. After all this, we would sit for our class – it would be 2 p.m. by then. It was understood that when I went there, I would spend the whole day there. But the benefit was that everyone at home spoke Urdu – that was also work for me, to understand the language. Khan Saheb didn't sit around quietly – he would recite some *shayari* (Urdu poetry). I was never disappointed that he wasn't teaching me, that I had gone all the way and I'm just sitting around. Nothing like that. It's important to get used to these things. You increase your patience, and you get the opportunity to learn.'

Though her association with Khan Saheb was for ten years, the time spent learning would have amounted to five years. Shubhaji went with the flow of Khan Saheb's wishes and moods. She remembers taking the entire family by double-decker bus to see the Gateway of India. During Muharram, music making stopped, but he would still insist that she come when they broke their fast. In the evenings, Khan Saheb and his sons would sing *marsiya*s while Shubhaji listened to all the festivities. 'I considered everything and decided that if this is what I'm to do, then I shouldn't create any trouble over things, or feel bad that I am paying fees and not getting to learn anything yet. I accepted this as part of the process.'

When Khan Saheb did teach Shubhaji, he was a very detail oriented and exacting teacher. The first challenge she encountered was his insistence that she stop learning from Shobhaji. 'If you want to learn my style, then you have to forget Shobhaji's style,' he told her. Shubhaji was deeply saddened by this, especially because Shobhaji's style had become so part of her voice and psyche. After some thought, she came to the conclusion that she would compartmentalize these styles: Shobhaji's music would remain in the original style, *ghazal*s would be in Khan Saheb's. When she told Shobhaji about Khan Saheb's request, she was encouraged to follow Khan Saheb's advice. 'You will benefit from this too,' Shobhaji told her. Though she stopped learning from Shobhaji during this period, she would visit her regularly.

The bulk of training in *ghazal* resided in mastering the compositions in all their nuance and glory. These compositions were embedded with varieties of *murki* and *khatka* ornaments that required a specific brand of vocal agility. The first step was training the voice to fit the mould of the *ghazal gayaki*. 'I had already begun giving many concerts professionally, so it was a big push to change my voice in the middle of my career. I was hanging somewhere between my original sound and this new style. I understood the difference, but it wasn't translating in my voice.'

Initially, Shubhaji found it difficult to reproduce the typical *khatka* of the *ghazal* – the difference being in the throw of the voice. In Shobhaji's style, the ornament was more open and raw, while in the *ghazal gayaki*, it was only partially open and the vocal throw required more restraint, softer volume, and a rounded phonetic.

Shubhaji attributes this difference in style to the context in which these styles developed. 'Music that evolved from the *kotha*s was entertainment that required a certain volume level, a certain clarity and openness of words so they are comprehensible. The *khatka*s and *murki*s also needed to be audible, then only they would get *daad* (vocal appreciation). Perhaps this is how that style developed. In this *ghazal gayaki*, the voice is thrown from the upper palate, and the pronunciations are half open, not full (*khula*). To modulate the voice, Khan Saheb would say, "Release the sound from your nose." Gradually, I listened to him and imitated his tone. It took me a long time to get control over this aspect of my voice. My voice was simply not moving in this direction, so I wondered how I would learn anything further.' But with time, Shubhaji's frustrations with her voice finally reached a place of personal satisfaction. Khan Saheb's training delivered a noticeable change in the balance of lightness and weight that she had been seeking.

Through the window of the composition, Shubhaji was also exposed to a different approach to raag, unlike what she had known thus far. Though *ghazal*s are based in classical raags, whether it is Charukesi or Bhairav, the presence of the raag is at the background, not the foreground as it is in classical rendition. 'All the raag elements are present, but you should only feel the shadow of the raag. This I learned from Khan Saheb – I didn't get this insight anywhere else.'

After decades of training in various forms, Shubhaji

believes in maintaining strict purity of each. She is not seeking to create a new identity or approach – for her, the beauty lies in being able to understand with depth the subtle differences that lie between *thumri*, *dadra*, *ghazal*, *bhajan*, and folk songs, and attain a high level of mastery over executing these. When classical singers attempt to present these forms, Shubhaji feels that many fall short in representing the styles authentically because their vocal inflections and pronunciations are classically oriented. She also feels that there is insufficient understanding around the required voice modulation to suit each form. 'Every aspect has to be learned. When I learned the folk style from my friend, Rajul, I had to understand how the words are thrown, how the voice is used. Folk music has its own *gayaki* and *bhav*. It's not enough to just throw the voice and sing loudly. These songs are *sufiyana* (centred around spiritual love). They are calling God, or a lover, or even putting a child to sleep. There is something to be said, a calling, and naturally this has its own *bhav*. None of these forms are without *bhav*, that has to be understood.' Even in the case of classical music, though it is shastra based, she insists that *bhav* must be at the forefront. 'Can any music exist without *bhav*?' she asks.

Shubhaji tells me the challenges she faced in getting concerts. Though she has toured internationally and performed around India, in general she found that organizers in India were heavily biased towards presenting classical music. 'My experience was that music circles were not interested in keeping anything other than classical.

I sing classical too, and in addition if I add *thumri* and *dadra*, these organizers label me as a *thumri* singer, not classical. I would tell them, I am trained in the Bhendi Bazaar gharana, and just like many classical singers sing *natyageet*, I sing *thumri* after my classical rendition. They don't understand *ghazal*, so I won't sing *ghazal*. I will present *thumri*, but they aren't interested. *Thumri* and *dadra* have their own dignity.'

To understand why this may be the case, it is necessary to view *thumri* and *dadra* (and its increasing absence from the music world) in the context of its history. These forms were mastered and popularized by the *tawaif*s, or courtesans, who were experts at music and dance entertainment in medieval courts and *kotha*s. Their association with sexual relations outside marriage resulted in denigration by the British rulers, as well as by upper-caste Indian Nationalist leaders, wiping out a generation of practitioners and torchbearers of the art form. Present-day beliefs around these genres have roots in the widespread propaganda that was based on the moral judgment of these artistes.

Shubhaji recounted the conditions in which this music was produced. 'In those times, *tawaif*s were very learned in music, having trained under great Ustads and done *riyaz* every day. They may have been called *kothewalis*, but they were truly singers. Later on, because of the kind of people who came to the *kotha*s to listen, their stature started to diminish. They had to add more elements of dance and other types of songs. But even these women had to fill their stomachs, earn their daily wage. They had to forget their classical roots, and the status of *thumri* and *dadra* also suffered. It did not command the respect it had previously. Because *thumri* was sung in the *kotha*, it has become secondary, *faltu*. This is not correct. Each form has its own standing. Whatever has reached us in the present-day, we must carefully take forward. If not, it will continue to diminish in importance and eventually die out.'

Shubhaji's reflections brought me back to the question of hierarchy and the use of the inaccurate term '*light* classical music.' It is evident from the rigorous training, thought, and effort that goes into mastering these genres that it is far from light. In many ways, these forms have a very different set of demands and skills than *khayal* music. These structures require mastery of multiple aesthetic frameworks, numerous languages, and varied vocal techniques. They require a certain brand of rebellious creativity (at times abandoning the boundaries of raag and taal), one that breaks the conventions followed in *khayal*. This freedom somehow feeds into a musical language that reaches more people. Perhaps, as Shubhaji suggests, these factors played a role in the hierarchization of the *thumri*, which reflected the bias against the 'type' of people who performed it, as well as the type of music that was performed.

At the level of the textual and the poetic, the feminist in me has at times felt uncomfortable with the lyrical content of the *thumri*, particularly the fact that women are usually depicted in the position of pining and waiting for their lover. Where was their agency? Why could it not be the other way around? When I ask Shubhaji about this, she attributes it to her idea of the fundamental nature of men and women. 'The woman is not secondary here, but ultimately it is women who show emotions. Yes, they are calling the lover, waiting for him, and after he comes, they have instructions of what he can and cannot do, where he cannot go, that he cannot go to his *sautan* (illicit lover). Because, generally men don't worry about where their beloved has gone, or how they can make their beloved comply.'

Perhaps because of the poetic subtext, as well as the aesthetics of the style, Shubhaji believes that *thumri* and *dadra* are suited best to the female voice. She does not enjoy male artistes' renditions, even those artistes that are considered to be among the greats. 'They sing in their *gayaki*, but that is not from the perspective of *thumri*.'

The *thumri* has always perplexed me. Is it the poetic and musical voice of women as conceived by men? Or is it that there is a 'woman's voice' that is different in *kind* from a male's voice? I have always been interested in the ways that voice gets gendered (an issue discussed earlier with Shubhada Paradkar in the context of the Agra gharana and Rumi Harish), and Shubhaji made me address a question that I had shied away from: how is it possible to conceptualize the gendered voice?

But my long discussions with her left me with new questions, ones that I hope I can explore through practice. How could I reconcile myself as a modern woman within a traditional art form that was created in a different cultural and historical context? Was it necessary to reimagine feminism, or reimagine the *thumri*? Is it appropriate or fair for a twenty-first century woman to view this art through the lens of contemporary feminism? And how have these forms been feminized, and therefore placed in hierarchies?

While spending time with Shubhaji, I realized that feminism cannot be contained within ideology or trends. Shubhaji embodies the lived experiences of her own brand of feminism that is rooted in action and bold choices. A self-made independent woman, choosing to sing the music of her choice at any cost and at a great investment of her time and effort, and achieving mastery of forms that required tremendous skill, intellect, and creativity. Perhaps feminism is the step that each woman takes to live her life on her own terms despite all odds, and Shubhaji is a living example of this.

9

YOGESH SAMSI

Recovering Lost Traditions

WHEN I MOVED TO BENGALURU IN 2003, THE PLAN for my first year of *talim* was clearly charted out by my guru, Aditi Upadhya. In addition to a rigorous schedule of training and practice, she insisted that I soak in the culture of Hindustani music by travelling around India to attend concerts and festivals. The best way to do this, she said, was to accompany her brother, Yogesh, a tabla artiste who was frequently on the concert circuit. As a complete ignoramus to the world of Hindustani music, during a time that was pre-YouTube and pre-Google, I obediently agreed. I had no idea about the stature of the artiste I would be travelling with, nor the musical universe I was about to enter.

I joined Yogesh Samsi in Mumbai as he travelled to various cities as a soloist and co-artiste with renowned vocalists. There were many stops on the itinerary: Aurangabad, Pune, Bhopal, Jalandhar, Bhaini Sahib,

Ludhiana. Modes of transport were many: train, flight, car, bus, even cycle rickshaw. I was a fly on the wall, silently sandwiched between students and admirers, organizers and impresarios. I sat through late-night festivals bundled up in shawls and a monkey cap, sipping steaming chai and nibbling delightfully flaky samosas as music blasted on Ahuja speakers in *pandal*s filled with tens of thousands of listeners. In Jalandhar, after Yogeshji played a late-night concert with vocalist Ajoy Chakrabarty, we were taken to one of his students' homes at 3 a.m., where I had the best alu paratha and lassi I have ever tasted.

Culinary joys aside, it was the music that wrapped itself around me like a comforting *razai* on a cold winter night in Punjab. In Aurangabad, I received my first glimpse into the virtuosity of my guru's brother during a tabla duet with Ustad Zakir Hussain. It was an open-air concert organized by the tourism department at the site of the famous Aurangabad caves. Crowds were teeming and security was tight, typical in a concert featuring Zakirji. I tried to remain inconspicuous in the tent that served as the green room, observing the banter between the artistes and the pre-concert buzz.

When the music began, it was a dance like I'd never seen before. A conversation of abstract rhythms that only heightened in intensity and expression. Though the tabla is typically seen in an accompanying role, it has a vast solo repertoire and a cultish following by percussion connoisseurs around the world. For the uninitiated, a tabla solo (or duet, in this case) can be exhilarating, perplexing and daunting. A typical recital features almost two hours of a gradual build-up of complex rhythmic patterns, starting with an abstract dance that carves different shapes in time, building to a frenzied height of energy, speed and patterns packaged densely at fractional intervals. The tabla solo is a peculiar creature full of contradictions: an act of individual expression that is at the same time fiercely loyal to tradition; an elastic exploration of the space between beats, but also of razor-sharp precise language patterns that have been passed down over generations. This balancing act between self and tradition, between improvised expression and prescription, reveals the virtuosity of a tabla artiste.

At the centre of it all is *upaj* – an exercise in spontaneity, creativity and alertness. A musical idea is born and it continues to grow and expand by a string of ex-tempo musical responses. The artiste follows the source idea with both courage and curiosity to wherever it may take him. He commits to the process without knowing the outcome, whether he is on the stage of a big auditorium or in the private confines of his home. It requires absolute presence of mind to ensure that a golden moment doesn't pass by unnoticed. *Upaj* thrives in the delight of risk and the unknown, a state of flow, trust and surrender. I was witnessing one musical leap of faith after another without a moment of pause. The thrill of the *upaj* process cannot be replicated or recreated – it is a shared roller-coaster ride between the artiste and the audience that happens in live performance, a hallmark of the Hindustani musical form. In this case, *upaj* was a conversation. I wondered how these musical giants could create that magic on demand in front of twenty thousand people. I returned to Bengaluru electrified, after realizing in small doses the musical magnitude of Yogesh Samsi.

—

Yogeshji's talent was discovered at the early age of two by his vocalist parents, Pandit Dinkar Kaikini and Vidushi Shashikala Kaikini. (He was legally adopted by his maternal grandfather, Dr Ratnakar Samsi, who had five daughters and wanted his name to live on. Hence, he does not use the surname Kaikini.) His father, a respected performer, composer and guru of the Agra gharana, came home one evening from work to find his youngest child cranky from a fever. Kaikiniji was an assistant producer for All India Radio in Delhi, and his duties included a detailed review of the National Programme broadcasts. He tuned in at home and tried to listen to the evening's artiste, Malabika Kanan, over the tantrum of his son Yogesh, who was insisting that somebody give him a tabla set to play. To appease him, Kaikiniji asked his wife to give the toddler the tabla so he could listen in peace. Kanan was performing raag Chhayanat and began a short *alap* before launching into the composition *Nevar ki jhankaar* in the taal *jhumra*, a less commonly sung rhythmic cycle of fourteen beats. Yogeshji, whose vocabulary at this time consisted of a few baby babbles, stood on his knees to reach the height of the two drums of the tabla set, placed his hands intuitively in the appropriate positions, and baffled his parents by playing tabla accompaniment for the entire broadcast performance in this complex rhythmic cycle with all the flourishes and nuances used by professional tabla artistes. His parents, stunned to tears, recognized an inexplicable gift in their child, which they would nurture and allow to take shape organically.

Kaikiniji taught his son the tabla basics he had learned as part of his vocal training – the various taal cycles (a fixed number of beats that repeat in a continuous cycle), different tabla compositions and phraseology. As a child, Yogeshji loved accompanying his mother while she sang, playing with her anytime he was asked to perform for guests or at family functions. His earliest memories of tabla were from an unusual perspective: lying on his mother's lap and watching her arms and fingers move as she played the *dagga* while teaching her students. While his toddler years were filled with memories of musical times in Delhi, the family eventually moved to Mumbai after Kaikiniji received an offer to become principal of Bharatiya Vidya Bhavan. Here, at the age of six, the young Yogesh began lessons with Pandit Taranath Rao Hattiangadi. However, this was disrupted after a short period of eight months, when Taranathji moved to the US to become a percussion faculty at CalArts University. It was only when he was nine that tabla training took a more formalized structure. A chance meeting occurred between Kaikiniji and Ustad Alla Rakha at a music patron's home, during which

Kaikiniji mentioned that he wanted his son to study with him. To formalize this request, Kaikiniji invited him to their home so he could meet and hear his son. Soon after, Abbaji (as Ustad Alla Rakha was fondly called) and his son, the tabla icon-to-be Zakir Hussain, came to the Kaikini household to assess this boy's potential as a *shishya*.

'I was nervous as hell,' Yogeshji recalls. He played a few pieces he had prepared, after which Abbaji recited different rhythmic patterns that he had to reproduce on the instrument. He increased the complexity of these and Yogeshji tried to keep up with his demands. With a reticence typical of musicians of his generation, Abbaji did not reveal his reaction to the child with much expression, concluding the audition by asking Kaikini to bring young Yogesh to their house later that week.

Yogeshji and his parents reached Abbaji's home on the planned date, only to find their house in a flurry of activity. Furniture was moved aside, many dressed up guests bustled about – it seemed like there was some sort of family celebration taking place and the Kaikinis were sure they had the date wrong.

Addressing Abbaji's wife, Kaikiniji asked, 'Ammaji, I hope we aren't intruding on a family function? Abbaji had asked us to come today.'

'No, no, absolutely not. This is certainly the right day!' she replied. 'We have prepared everything for the *ganda bandhan* ceremony for Yogesh,' she said, referring to the traditional ceremony that cements the relation of guru to disciple. For some reason, perhaps not to impose on the Kaikini family's modest lifestyle, Abbaji hadn't told them of his plans to host an elaborate gathering that included family, students, and respected members of the musical community as witnesses. The living room at their residence in Simla House was packed with artistes – sarangi virtuoso Sultan Khan, Kathak exponent Sitara Devi, and Zakir Hussain and his siblings Fazal, Taufiq, and Razia. As typically done in the ritual, first the guru recites a prayer, and then the guru and shishya feed each other jaggery and chickpeas. This is followed by a lesson in front of all guests to symbolize the beginning of this lifelong relationship. The Kaikinis were shocked by the extensive preparations that were made unbeknownst to them, and it became very clear that Abbaji saw exceptional potential in their son.

Ustad Allah Rakha Qureshi was born in Jammu during the era of the British Raj (1919), and like many great artistes of his era, he left home at the young age of twelve to follow his calling to be a musician. He found his guru, Mian Qadir Baksh II, in Lahore in 1931. Baksh was considered the *khalifa* (the last surviving Ustad of the family) of the Punjab gharana of tabla at the time. In the world of tabla, there are six main schools (gharanas) of thought: Delhi, Lucknow, Farukkhabad, Ajrada, Benares, and Punjab. The idiom of the Punjab gharana is derived from the rhythmic language, or *bhasha*, of the pakhavaj (a barrel shaped two-headed drum) and jori (a pakhavaj inspired two drum instrument used in the Sikh community), both known for resonant and powerful open strokes.

Baksh was a demanding guru who followed the traditional gurukul model. Abbaji was responsible for all his guru's needs including domestic chores and daily cooking of all meals. A towering figure at six feet, legend has it that Baksh had an insatiable appetite that required a heavy rotation of varieties of meat dishes. At the end of a long day, if he was in the mood, he would decide to teach Abbaji from 11 p.m. onwards. Whether the lessons occurred or not, Abbaji's *riyaz* regimen was rigorous and unflagging. His *talim* lasted for approximately nine years in this fashion, during which he received valuable nuggets of repertoire.

However, history would change the trajectory and musical evolution of the Punjab gharana. While all the other gharanas remained unaffected by the new borders of Partition as they were based in Uttar Pradesh, the Punjab gharana faced the prospects of division. Post Partition, most gharana musicians, including Baksh, remained in Pakistan. Thus, only tabla players living in Pakistan could receive his training, as travelling across the border for *talim* was too risky. Musicians of the other major tabla gharanas remained in post-independence India, where knowledge dissemination and propagation allowed styles to flourish and information to exchange freely. By this time, Abbaji had moved to Mumbai, where he was employed as an artiste for All India Radio. As one of the few practitioners of the Punjab gharana style in India, and also as an individualistic innovator, he evolved a very specific stream of thought.

'The *parampara* of Punjab that Abbaji established here in India is his own, totally reborn. In those days the great pillars of tabla who had already emerged on the scene were taking the whole world of tabla by storm. For him to work his way through in those days as a young, emerging, thinking, creative tabla player, and to make his mark on the scene was very challenging. I would say his thought process was much ahead of his time. As a result, he faced criticism by the traditionalists of those days, including prominent musicians. This was not because he wasn't playing the right kind of tabla. It was because people found it hard to comprehend his thought process, and also didn't have the idea that there is really no label of right or wrong in art and that it's just one's perspective,' Yogeshji reflects.

Abbaji's style built upon his Punjab foundations, in which he eventually conceptualized a very unique perspective of *peshkar* (a section of slower and free explorations of the rhythm cycle), *qaida* (a structure that is improvised upon as a theme and variation), and *tihai* (patterns repeated in groups of three). He added his own layer of thought to these elements by going deeper into the complexity of *laya* and the division of time in the taal cycle. Breaking out of even divisions of the cycle, Abbaji often explored uneven and fractional divisions of space, overlapping *avartans* (rhythm cycles), playing with offbeat and on beat accents, returning to the beat in the most unexpected ways. At the time, his solos were attended by many tabla players who were curious to understand these new approaches to *laya* improvisation and developing a tabla solo.

'I must say that Abbaji started another branch of Punjab gharana philosophy – that's what he gave birth to. There is nobody who has played that style of tabla apart from his disciples, Zakir bhai and us. He introduced the world to so many ways of thinking about language, different dimensions to accompaniment and improvisation,' Yogeshji says.

At his home, Abbaji could almost always be seen tapping his thumb against his fingers, a typical mannerism of counting used by tabla players. However, in Abbaji's case, this was a non-stop state of mind, whether the TV was on or guests were visiting. Yogeshji saw this first hand many times. 'He was always creating something, it was a state of meditation. His subconscious was in a state of dormant creation all the time. I've seen him like that.'

When Yogeshji began training under Abbaji, it was physically and mentally rigorous and exhausting, and he took time to adjust to the demands and pace of learning. Teaching him in the enclosed balcony of his Malabar Hill flat, Abbaji would ask the young boy to come several days a week to sit for extended lessons of two to three hours, after which he would ask Yogeshji to go down to his garage to practise what had been taught. This allowed him to monitor his practice habits closely and occasionally intervene. The garage functioned as a gurukul of sorts – it had been converted into a practice space for all students. Many of them, including Yogeshji, have spent hours toiling there. By evening, Abbaji would make his way down to the garage to make any corrections.

On some evenings, after hearing Yogeshji's practice in the garage, Abbaji would go back upstairs to his home for his own *riyaz* with a nagma player (melodic accompaniment provided to a tabla solo), asking him to come along to listen and closely observe these sessions. Many times, after the nagma player left, around 8.30 p.m., Abbaji would launch into another lesson with Yogeshji, sometimes going on until 11 p.m. 'This whole process included him teaching and playing in front of me, doing his *riyaz*, sometimes allowing me to play along with him – this ended up being like a gurukul system. I was not living there, but all practical purposes of the gurukul were covered.'

He received countless hours of *seena-ba-seena* training, notwithstanding a full school schedule. On the very rare occasion when he missed a class due to exams, Abbaji called his mother and gave her an earful for not sending him. In their classes, Abbaji would spend large chunks of time only on *padhant*, the recitation of the rhythmic patterns, before Yogeshji was allowed to attempt playing on the instrument. He demanded unwavering alertness – when a concept was shared it had to be replicated immediately without error, and as Abbaji kept developing the idea, he was expected to keep up and replicate the entire progression of thought, Abbaji's *upaj*.

'Abbaji's *vistar* (rhythmic development) used to go over my head and took me months to decipher. If I couldn't follow his thought, he used to get very frustrated and lose his temper with me. His teaching style was non-stop *padhant*, and I just had to pick it up on the spot. No questions, no analysis. I had to go home and think about it – for instance, why is this rhythmic sentence overlapping and going into the next part of the taal cycle? I was used to listening to patterns of four all the time, so overlapping over that space initially sounded very strange. But when I started getting the hang of it within the frame of the taal cycle, it sounded incredible, because that idea was itself a beautiful novel creation. You can only appreciate it when you have command over the underlying taal, not if you lose that grip. This is just a small example of how I would unpack, analyze, and dissect every difficulty that I faced with him. And then I would assimilate those concepts and put them together to do a complete *riyaz* to try to see the musical and lyrical flow. The pace and energy of *talim* that happened continuously in this manner for years. The process eventually answered all my questions and cleared all my doubts over the next decade. In those days, this was typically how *seena-ba-seena talim* happened,' Yogeshji recalls.

Talim also included an exchange of anecdotes that unraveled kernels of wisdom. Abbaji would share his experiences of playing with Pandit Ravi Shankar, many of which inspired him to think about his approach to tabla solo in different ways. 'Abbaji gives a lot of credit to Ravi Shankarji for having given him opportunities to play in different time cycles, like *tisra jati rupak* (a seven-beat cycle sub-divided into triplets), *matta* taal, *char* taal *ki savari, pancham savari,* etc. Abbaji got opportunities to think, create and find ways through these cycles. That became a process of evolution for him.'

The biggest takeaway from playing unusual and rare taals was the ability to adapt phrases into different rhythm cycles. 'If I need to use a specific phrase in a different taal than what I am used to, how can I make it sound grammatically complete, poetic, and still fit the division of that taal, or the *farashbandi* of that taal? How can a phrase of eight get constructed as seven and a half? If it's Rupak (cycle of seven), then how can it be divided as three and a half and three and a half? These are the things we used to discuss, and these became the gospel of *sutra*s for me: how to convert *qaida*s to different taals, how to treat phrases in different taals, how to deal with the language. I learned that *qaida* compositions don't inherently belong to any taal, but they can be poetically adapted to any taal. This thought process became a whole new world. I had started playing tabla solos in different taals, so he considered me mature enough to discuss these things. *Talim* happened at so many tiers with him. And though every stage of *talim* had its role to play in my development as an artiste – the last ten years were like a crown on the king's head. There were so many small but very significant ideas and thought processes about *vistar*, accompaniment, about solo, so many little things that we shared, just through discussion and *padhant*.

'Towards the end of my *talim* (training), my brain was working faster and I was able to retain a lot of his ideas. These were days when we didn't have the luxury of buying a walkman to record the class. I was not even allowed to keep a notebook. In fact he hated seeing me with a book and pen and never allowed me to write anything down. Later on, because he realized he was forgetting, he would ask me to write after the lesson was over. Though I made an effort to write everything, after a point I used to give up because his *talim* moved at such a ferocious velocity that there was no point in writing anything down. It was better to retain, go home and write down whatever was possible, and spend most of my time thinking about it. This became a habit – to make the cerebral intellectual process the main forte of creation. Otherwise it became "by hearted" tabla. This made my brain work on overdrive, and this process of self-analysis actually put me on the path to free improvisation over the next fifteen to twenty years.'

At this stage of his career, Abbaji had stopped performing, so *talim* happened at a theoretical and practical level at his home. To observe the on-stage application of these thoughts, Yogeshji followed Zakir Hussain's winter concerts in India very closely. Here, the seeds of his *talim* would bloom in the most unexpected and splendorous forms. 'Everything came alive for me as a young tabla player and upcoming artiste when I heard

Zakir bhai. All the creative ideas that Abbaji shared in the last 10 years came alive on the stage, because I could understand what he was trying to say through Zakir bhai's playing.'

The winter music season in Mumbai during the 1970s and 1980s still retained an intimacy of medium scale venues, baithaks, as well as large scale festivals. Discerning listeners flocked to witness their favourite artistes in close quarters. 'I have heard Zakir Bhai in such settings hundreds of times. At the peak of Abbaji's accompaniment career, he started a novel idea of finishing his *tihai* on the point where the *mukhda* (beginning of the composition) started. (Typically, these patterns finish on the first beat of the rhythmic cycle.) Now this practice has become common, and has taken the entire accompaniment world by storm. Abbaji started the trend and Zakir bhai has taken it to unimaginable heights. Almost every single time I heard Zakir Bhai, his playing used to be packed with intellectual depth. I used to feel – how does he do it, and when is that day going to come when I can do even fifteen percent of this? It was a source of inspiration. It used to pump me up to try to strive for more, to strive for that depth of knowledge.'

Outside his training with Ustad Alla Rakha, Yogeshji was receiving a parallel education in the art of accompaniment, a starkly different skill and mindset from solo playing, though based on the same building blocks. Every night, from the age of twelve, he accompanied his father's *riyaz*, simultaneously developing a deep understanding of the nuances of the vocal music that had been a fixture in his household since his birth. His father taught him the aesthetic value of *shuddh theka*, or the pure, unadorned rhythmic syllables of the taal. When the need for embellishment arose, Kaikiniji guided his son by suggesting what types would be aesthetically suitable and at which point in the rendition they would be appropriate.

'The most important thing is to realize how much you're supposed to give at a specific point of time in a rendition. If you're not comfortable sacrificing as an accompanist, then your musicianship starts becoming questionable,' he says, referring to the choice of prioritizing self-interest over the larger musical decision that the moment may demand. 'These are the things my father shared with me,' he recalls.

With decades of daily *saath sangat* (accompaniment) practice with his father, Yogeshji honed an asset that is rare for tabla players: an equal command over accompaniment and solo playing. By the age of eighteen, Pandit K.G. Ginde insisted on taking the young teenager for a commercial recording for HMV, after which Yogeshji travelled on tour with his father to the United States in 1986. Yogeshji's tonal quality, meditative steadiness of tempo, selective restraint in embellishment, and high energy and thoughtful creative interjections when demanded, were sought after qualities. In his early twenties, he was accompanying artistes like Shubhada Paradkar, Shruti Sadolikar, Ulhas Bapat, D.K. Datar, and N. Rajam. Eventually, superstar musicians Shivkumar Sharma and Hariprasad Chaurasia would ask him to accompany them regularly, and his career trajectory would explode.

The nuance of accompaniment boils down to the notion of *theka* – a fixed string of rhythmic syllables that come together to define a particular taal. It is the essential base structure upon which tabla artistes improvise, sometimes by filling in the spaces between beats, playing with tonal quality and resonance, or by embellishing syllables as per their own taste. The tabla player is expected to be a chameleon – blending the style of playing to match the aesthetic of the vocalist or instrumentalist. While vocalists of certain styles prefer an austere, unornamented *theka*, others may prefer the tabla player to engage more aggressively with the space of the taal cycle by deviating from the *theka* for certain stretches of improvisation and then returning back to the original form. A thoughtful tabla player would be sensitized to these often unspoken requirements and quick to respond in the moment.

Many of Yogeshji's reflections on the aesthetic choices of accompaniment came from his interactions with his father, as well as a great deal of introspection. 'I realized that I needed to think about how I could play a non-monotonous *theka*, to make it artistically interesting. In vocal music, each *avartan* (rhythmic cycle) should be according to how the *khayal* is being expanded. What syllables are appropriate to prefix and suffix a phrase?

What syllables should I use if I want to present slightly longer phrases? I used to reflect and do a lot of listening, ear training. That helped me work out my own style and perspective of accompanying vocal music. And I realized that as much as I thought about tabla solo, I have probably thought about accompaniment even more, because accompaniment can never be taught. While tabla solo can be taught, accompaniment cannot because you never know what situation you're going to encounter, and hence it is a continuous process of discovery and realization,' he says.

In the context of instrumental music, Yogeshji credits his long association with Pandit Shivkumar Sharma for shaping his style, thought process, and aesthetics. 'Because he was a tabla player himself initially, he could really nurture me through the finer aspects of accompaniment in instrumental music. We discussed how to maintain the steadiness of *theka* while expressing myself freely, and how to gel with the artiste. We spent a lot of time speaking about these things, and those inputs really opened up a lot of perspective in instrumental music accompaniment.'

Yogeshji steadily rose through the ranks of the tabla world, from being a sensitive accompanist before also being sought after as a soloist. 'There were hardly any solo concerts in those days,' he recalls. But as opportunities arose, he made an impression as an independent thinker steeped in Ustad Alla Rakha's concepts.

At this point in his career, his solos attracted their own following, and many times Abbaji would make it a point to attend as well. 'When I used to tell him I was performing, he would ask for the time and place and traveled far just to listen to me. In the last ten years of my *talim*, a period that went at a deeply intellectual level, he used to especially like to come and listen to my solos. At this stage, I used to do a lot of things in my own little vision and insight that I got in my *vistar*. He used to acknowledge that risk and appreciate it. It gave me an extremely satisfying feeling of acceptance in my heart that he probably thought that I'm on the right path,' he remembers.

On February 2, 2000, the Qureshi family faced an unspeakable tragedy when they lost their daughter, Razia. Within twenty-four hours of hearing this news, at the age of eighty, Abbaji suffered a fatal heart attack. Fate would have it that he would breathe his last breath in Yogeshji's arms, an epochal moment of guru resigning to his *shishya*.

—

After twenty-three years of intensely close association – a bond of choice perhaps stronger than blood – Yogeshji was left without a guru. He struggled to face a world without Abbaji, at the same time feeling his presence in every stroke and phrase he produced. He says, 'There was a time when it became difficult for me to understand how I would converse with anybody at that level. It was just not possible.'

But his life followed a lived *upaj* sequence of its own. In 2006 in Jawaddi Taksal, a village nestled in Ludhiana,

Yogeshji made his way through the confused blend of idolatrous hospitality and chaotic disorganization that characterizes many classical music concerts in India. It was momentous to have an internationally reputed tabla player and disciple of the legendary Ustad Alla Rakha visit Jawaddi Taksal for a solo tabla recital at the Gurudwara.

Yogeshji reached the venue, but his harmonium accompanist was nowhere to be found. A tabla solo is always accompanied by a one-line melody that serves the function of holding the beat and tempo from start to finish, usually provided by a harmonium or sarangi. In a communication snafu, the presenters didn't realize that they were responsible for booking the accompanist. Meanwhile, the Gurudwara was teeming with an audience, including tabla professionals and students who had traveled from other villages in Punjab just to hear him. A tall, wiry man sporting a safari suit, full-rim square spectacles and hair slicked back with oil, came up to Yogeshji with a request: 'We've all come to listen to you and there's no one to play with you. If you don't mind, can I play with you? My name is Sushil Kumar Jain.' Left with no other choice, Yogeshji took a chance and agreed to perform with him and see where the evening would go. The seemingly simple task of providing the repeated melodic line, the *nagma*, is in fact a great feat – a tight-rope walk of maintaining a steady tempo while the tabla player dives and dodges between micro-beats of varying fractions.

It became apparent that Jain Saheb, as the elder man was respectfully addressed, was unlike the typically calm and composed *nagma* artiste. A crackling live wire ran through his body from the moment his fingers touched the harmonium. When Yogeshji started playing, his body did its own dance, moving and responding to each turn of beat.

Yogeshji was in the middle of a *rela*, a fast-paced densely packed composition with ongoing improvised variations, when Jain Saheb uncontrollably clasped his wrist. Yogeshji came to a sudden halt, figuring that there must be a problem with the sound. 'I'm so sorry to interrupt you, but can I say something about Abbaji?' he said. Yogeshji, mid-solo, was taken aback by the sudden mention of his guru but asked him to proceed.

'I never realized that I would be reminded of Abbaji like this again in my life. I want to say something about Abbaji that I wrote when he passed away in 2000.'

Jain Saheb proceeded to recite a poem which fused rhythmic tabla syllables with Urdu poetry in praise and remembrance of the tabla stalwart on the morning of his passing. In that moment, Yogeshji realized that Jain Saheb had a gift, and an undeniable energy of tabla pulsating through his body.

This was no ordinary man, nor was their meeting a mere accident.

After the concert, it was decided that the two musicians would travel together the next day and Yogeshji would drop Jain Saheb off at his home in Chandigarh on the way to the airport. The three-hour ride from Jawaddi to Chandigarh packed even more intensity and ferocity of rhythmic exchange than the previous evening. 'Will you recite some of Abbaji's compositions for me? I would like to understand them,' he requested. What began was a *padhant* repartee, a verbal recitation of these tabla compositions, each one inspiring the next in a domino effect. Soon, Jain Saheb took over and single handedly recited a storehouse of repertoire Yogeshji had never heard before for two straight hours.

They reached Chandigarh early, allowing a bit of time for Yogeshji to visit Jain Saheb's home before heading to the airport. They exchanged formalities over tea, but it was not long before the conversation came back to music. In the music room, Yogeshji asked the question that he had been mulling over for the past few hours. 'Will you teach me these compositions?' The sprightly man bounced like a spring from the floor, gathered three thick ledgers from his cupboard and placed them on Yogeshji's lap. 'Take these with you. They are all yours,' he said without a second thought. The books were filled with rare compositions of the Punjab gharana and Jain Saheb's own creations, undiscovered gems – a peculiar vocabulary and idiom that had not been part of the popularly performed repertoire. Yogeshji realized that he had fortuitously stumbled upon a hidden treasure; a sharp, fertile, creative intellect with deep knowledge in *shastra*. Few individuals in the sub-continent possessed this material, most of which was lost when many gharana musicians settled in Pakistan after Partition. In the trauma of Partition and its aftermath, this tradition of music was also a victim.

'Jain Saheb, it's not possible for me to learn from books, because I've never done that,' Yogeshji explained. 'Abbaji never taught me from a book, and in twenty three years of training he didn't even allow me to write anything down. I've always taken *seena-ba-seena talim* and I firmly believe in the value of that. So I will take the time out and come here. I will stay near your house and come and learn from you properly, *seena-ba-seena,*' he told him, upon which Jain Saheb became very emotional. A new thread was being woven into the historical fabric of the Punjab gharana.

After that meeting, Yogeshji began visiting Jain Saheb to sit with him face to face and learn these rare compositions. He found an entire range of possibilities in these new usages in language and expression, specifically the unique grouping of syllables in combinations that were less commonly heard. The beauty lay in adapting these syllables to the tabla, in which the sound has the capacity to maintain the vigor of the pakhavaj while adding soft and ringing timbres, thereby expanding its soundscape.

Jain Saheb's ledgers contained scores of compositions that played with different pairings and combinations of these rare syllables, arranged in complex varieties of rhythmic metre. His own musical history is layered and fraught with inexplicable obstacles. His talent and passion for tabla from a young age was relegated to the sphere of hobby. Due to lack of family support to pursue it as a profession, he would eventually work as a bank clerk at Union Bank. He studied under Pandit Naurata Ram Mohan – a tabla player who also directed a theatre company based on classical music – and later under Acharya Lachman Singh Seen, disciple of Ustad Mian Qadar Baksh. He was also enriched by many encounters with musicians of the gharana who lived in Punjab or would visit from Pakistan.

After his fated encounter with Yogeshji, he had finally found a person who not only revered the value of his knowledge and collection, but also drew great inspiration from his own original compositions and creativity. His treasure trove of ledgers included his own compositions, many of which he attributes to the divine inspiration of great masters of the gharana. The mystical elements of his creative process are part of Jain Saheb's aura – a man with a special connection to the tabla cosmos, regaining bits of lost history and creating anew within tradition.

It's the spring of 2000, and Yogeshji is in San Francisco watching the *X-Files* movie with Zakirji. They are the only two people in the entire theatre. Meetings with Zakirji are organic and spontaneous. The two artistes happened to have a common window of free time while Yogeshji was touring the US. When he found out about the opening in his schedule, he hopped on a flight and spent three days alone with the maestro, an opportunity that would be unlikely to present itself in India.

Over a burrito and coke, they talked shop, listened to Mehdi Hasan until three in the morning, and chatted about the musicians that had impacted their lives. Zakirji spoke about the critical role Ustad Ali Akbar Khan played in liberating him from planned music to creating with freedom on stage – sitting on the stage with an empty and fertile mind. By the third day, after many musical topics had been exhausted, Yogeshji expressed his desire to gain insight into Zakirji's thought processes. They started at three in the afternoon, exploring Zakirji's own compositions and improvisation techniques. Delving deeper into how he thinks, Yogeshji showed him his way of applying these concepts. Zakirji also shared his ideas about accompaniment, demonstrating how he thinks about sentence improvisation in *saath sangat*, how he forms *tihai*s on the spot, and how he judges the main artiste's creative process while accompanying, to support and not overpower.

The topic of discussion returned to their first ever duet concert in Aurangabad, in 1997. This concert, which would be a significant moment in Yogeshji's career, was in fact never planned. Though he had initially attended the concert as a listener, Zakirji learned of his presence and asked him to accompany him on the spot. On stage, what emerged was an enthralling duet. 'That concert was more of a practical sharing of ideas – I was trying to play per my own thought process and he played per his. In this massive six hour session, we thrashed out everything that happened in that Aurangabad solo that had been on my mind. All the questions I needed to ask him started striking me. Between that solo experience, and then this discussion three years later in San Francisco, my outlook and approach was transformed. It was like *talim* of several years concentrated in a crash course. It still lives fresh in my memory.'

Their time together became even more precious in light of Zakirji's passing in 2024. This was a profound and personal loss for Yogeshji – Zakirji was his idol, a creative maverick, an older brother, and a friend. 'He was god's most spectacular creation that walked on this earth in the field of music, and especially tabla.'

Hindustani musicians often make the statement that they are lifelong students. It can come across as clichéd, or a display of false humility. But when I hear Yogeshji speak about the various ways in which he continues to seek and assimilate knowledge, the sheer immensity of learning is unmistakable. What does it mean to learn, and how do so many sources of information amalgamate into an art steeped in tradition while very much embracing change? Most often tradition is placed in opposition to modernity, as tradition seems to be unchanging while modernity offers a constant potential of change. However, the spirit of Hindustani music, both in vocal music as well as instrumental, is defined by change and improvisation.

To understand the idea of learning, I watched Yogeshji teach. I sat in on many of his lessons and workshops, soaked in the intensity of the energy exchange between guru and shishya, often hours of unbroken concentration and an unquenchable desire to achieve mastery. He only teaches full-time professional tabla players, many of whom are highly sought after young artistes. These lessons sometimes appear to continue like an unending volley between tennis greats, as many of Yogeshji's students respond with great alacrity to his challenges and are able to keep up with his pace of ideation. In one of his yearly workshops, a group of almost fifty tabla students followed the various steps of his improvisational creative journey. For the first four hours of playing, not a single word was uttered – only the language of tabla resonated throughout the hall in complete unison, a communal spirit of learning, focus, and brotherhood (almost all the students were males).

Yogeshji is a very dedicated teacher. 'My vision is very simple. My attitude towards teaching is the way I experienced my gurus. I teach with no compromise, and I don't hold anything back, because I believe that *vidya* has to be transmitted totally. I believe that the next generation must go ahead and excel far better than our generation. Don't teach with the insecurity that the student may go a few notches ahead. I have seen in front of my eyes gurus who teach students in a very measured way, because they feel too much is not to be given at a time or the student will excel them. It all depends on the level of the student. That has never been my thing. Only people like us can make an effort to make students realize the true value of tradition, without compromise. Once they're on the stage, there shouldn't be any compromise. They have a huge responsibility. In the initial part of your career when you face the stage, you must feel the weight. That keeps you grounded, that makes you think, that makes you introspect. That makes you come out stronger the next time because you can bear that weight. Initially you'll find yourself weak. The next time you will be stronger, the weight will become less. But one has to go through that process.'

While he believes in making the transfer of knowledge a transparent and honest exchange, he also realizes that learning conditions in the modern context have become much more comfortable. 'The garage at Abbaji's flat where I used to practise didn't even have a fan. The sweltering heat of summer in Mumbai can really squeeze out the last ounce of energy from your body. Sometimes during Eid there was a goat tied there. Today we sit in the comfort of luxurious spaces for *riyaz*, but we didn't have any of those. Students should understand how physically challenging the conditions were in those days.'

Yet, he believes the grit and character that old-style training instilled are also essential experiences for making music that comes from the soul. 'This process was what brought about the deepest emotions of an artiste. It's not only about *talim*, it's about how you have experienced life, challenged in situations on a day to day basis. It was a constant process of overcoming challenges. That makes you really feel that emotion intensely – when you want something really badly and it comes after a couple of decades, it's a whole different feeling. It's not about earning money, it's about reaching that level of execution of that one little phrase. It made you stronger. These things stir your heart, keep you grounded, keep you humble, because you never forget where you come from.'

I often drop by Yogeshji's hundred-year-old home in the tree filled side lanes of Gamdevi, Mumbai, tucked amidst constant honking and traffic. He is usually in his own zone of stillness and thought. His own *riyaz*, hectic performing, travel, and teaching schedule leave him little time to think about matters not related to his music. Students drop in and out of his house at any time – it is an open-door policy. I think about how these students, foot soldiers of the tradition, are shaping their identities as individual musicians as well as adding their ideas to a tradition lost, regained, and innovated. Rather than fossilizing the knowledge into an artifact, they have the responsibility of transforming it into a living, breathing, and evolving art of the present. Like Yogeshji, each will have to find a way to be liberated, rather than confined, by the legacy that bears the weight of a complex history. It is an uncontainable heritage that has shown that perhaps an essential ingredient of the creative experiment is the mystical – the association with a master guru, the guiding wisdom of a messenger, and a human vessel to radiate the message with an inextinguishable luminosity.

Acknowledgements

I AM VERY GRATEFUL TO MANY DIFFERENT PEOPLE FOR their support in making this book a reality.

To the artists featured in this book, my deep gratitude to you for trusting me to tell the stories of your personal journeys.

After sharing a sample stand-alone essay with the lovely Nisha Susan, a writer whose work I admire, she suggested that I write a collection of essays on Hindustani musicians in book format. The thought had never crossed my mind before, and I am truly grateful for her generosity of spirit and encouragement.

I am fortunate to have worked with Jayapriya Vasudevan and Radhika Shah at Jacaranda Literary Agency. They have been deeply understanding and patient through the entire process, always advocating on my behalf. It has been such a pleasure to get to know them through this process. Many thanks to Abhivyakti Singh, my sensitive and meticulous editor at Hachette, who gently guided me through the process.

As I mentioned in the Introduction, I owe everything to my gurus, Aditi Upadhya and Sudhindra Bhaumik.

I have also had the privilege of training under the late Pandit Dinkar Kaikini and Smt Shashikala Kaikini, and I'm deeply indebted to them for their generosity. Without all of them, I would have the least inkling about the world or culture of Hindustani music. They have always supported my interest in exploring the field of music outside of performance, whether through writing or research. Beyond music, they have been sources of strength in my life. My gratitude also to Yogesh and Kavita Samsi for extending themselves to me musically and personally.

There were moments when I could not imagine that I would be able to complete this project. Had it not been for the support of my entire family, I do not think it would have been possible. The unwavering support of my parents, Ramaa and Sampath, has anchored me through difficult times. Their belief in me has kept me afloat when I couldn't muster it myself. My uncle and aunt, Sundar and Dhanu, have been important personal and intellectual figures in my growth since my childhood. Sundar has always been an essential sounding board and his feedback was critical in keeping this book true to its spirit and vision.

In the middle of writing this book, I moved to Mumbai, and I have been deeply grateful for the love and support I've received from Ritu, Nikhil, Aadya, and Vivaan Joshi.

I logged many hours of overseas and local phone calls and text messages with friends and family who listened to me with untiring patience: Ajay, Bindu, Gaurav, Nikki, Rebecca, Vyju. You fill my heart. I am also incredibly grateful for the support and guidance of Sonal Kothari over the years.

My thanks to the Brooklyn Raga Massive Artist Residency programme for the opportunity to work on certain sections of this book at the Rockefeller Pocantico Center amidst the company and conversations of a wonderful group of Hindustani musicians.

Thanks also to Shruteendra Katagade, Devina Dutt, and Sraboni Chaudhuri for facilitating meetings with artists and helpful conversations around music, musicians, and the larger music ecosystem.

And thanks to you, the reader, for taking the time to read this collection.

Glossary

***alap (ālāp)*:** an abstract improvised melodic exploration of a raag, using vowels and select consonants as phonetic vehicles. It is not set to a concrete rhythmic meter, though it has an abstract pacing and inherent movement.

***andolan (āndolan)*:** precise oscillating movement between two notes, slower in movement, often touching microtones used in the context of the raag.

***bada khayal (baḍā khayāl)*:** slow tempo composition in the *khayal* genre, typically comprised of two verses. Used interchangeably with *vilambit khayal*.

***bandish (bandiś)*:** compositional structure in the *khayal* style in which lyrics are placed within the frameworks of raag (melodic scale) and taal (rhythm cycle). Used interchangeably with *khayal* or *cheez*.

***baithak*:** an intimate concert in which the artist and audience are at close proximity, seated on the floor.

***chalan (calan)*:** arrangement and pacing of musical phrases in the context of a raag.

***chhota khayal* (*choṭā khayāl*)**: faster tempo composition in the *khayal* genre, typically comprised of two verses. Used interchangeably with *drut khayal*.

***dadra* (*dādrā*)**: compositional form in the semi-classical genre, typically sung in a medium or fast tempo in the six-beat *dadra* taal or eight-beat *keherva* taal. Themes are usually centered around love, separation from the beloved, and moods of the seasons.

dhrupad: style and compositional form of Hindustani classical music. Performance of dhrupad involves a detailed *nom tom alap*, followed by a fixed composition (typically four verses) that is developed with rhythmic improvisation.

gat: compositional structure set in a particular raag and taal. The term is typically used for instrumental music.

gamak: musical ornament that involves oscillation between two notes at a fast pace.

***gayaki* (*gāyakī*)**: style and features of a particular artist, specific to vocal music. This can be gharana related or individualistically developed.

***gharana* (*gharānā*)**: school of thought and associated stylistic features, specifically in the Hindustani classical music system. Rooted in the word *ghar* (home), as the music was traditionally passed down within families from fathers to sons. There are several prominent gharanas in classical vocal and instrumental music as well as in kathak.

gurukul: residential method of learning in which the student lives with the guru for immersive training.

jhala (jhālā): fast tempo section of development in instrumental music that follows *alap* and *jod*. Rhythmically driven, though not bound by taal, it is the concluding section of open raga development.

jod (joḍ): second section of free raag exploration in instrumental music. A moderately paced rhythmic metre is introduced.

khayal (khayāl): genre of Hindustani classical vocal music centred around improvised development of a raag within the context of *alap* and composition. *Khayal* also refers to the composition itself.

khatka (khatkā): musical ornament that involves repeated and fast movement around a central note.

laya: referring to speed, pace, timing, or any type of movement, depending on the context.

laykari (laykārī): playful division of space within a taal cycle, utilizing different subdivisions of microbeats to create moments of tension and release within the development of a composition.

meend (mīnḍ): gliding movement between two notes, varying curvature and microtonal usage depending contextually on the raag.

mehfil (maḥfil): musical or cultural gathering; often intimate, like a chamber concert.

***murchana* (*mūrcchanā*):** the process of transposing notes, maintaining equal intervals while shifting the base note, *sa*, to create new scales.

***murki*:** a delicate ornament that is a fast turn of notes, usually in a cluster.

***nom tom alap* (*nom tom ālāp*):** gradual and detailed form of free raag exploration in vocal music consisting of four parts of development. The first two parts, *sthayee* and *antara*, explore the lower and upper half of the raag scale, respectively. The third part, *sanchari*, introduces a rhythmic meter in a medium pace, while the fourth part, *abhog*, increases the pace and creates a climactic ending. The *nom tom alap* utilizes phonetic syllables like *ri*, *re*, *ta*, *na num*, and *nom* throughout. It originates from the *dhrupad* genre and is also practiced by *khayal* singers of the Agra gharana with style specific modifications.

***parampara* (*paramparā*):** unbroken lineage of gurus and disciples, spanning multiple generations.

***peshkar* (*peśkār*):** introductory section of tabla solo in which the *taal* cycle is explored in a slow tempo using the basic syllables of the theka. The structure includes a fixed theme that is explored through gradual stages of improvisation, finishing with a peshkar qaida.

***pukaar* (*pukār*):** throw of voice that is characterized by expressiveness and a particular emotional charge.

qaida: a composed structure for tabla in the form of a couplet. It is improvised with multiple variations based on various permutations and combinations of the syllables used in the couplet.

***raag* (*rāg*)/ *raga* (*rāgā*)**: melodic structure based on a fixed scale of notes, arranged in a particular sequence, defined by characteristic phrases, pacing, and a particular mood.

***riyaz* (*riyāz*)**: term used for practice in Hindustani music.

***sadhana* (*sādhanā*)**: deep practice and way of living that implies a level of focus and immersion in a subject over a long period of time.

***sanskar* (*sanskār*)**: in the context of music, refers to musical and cultural exposure as part of upbringing.

***shruti* (*śruti*)**: microtones, small perceivable intervals of tone. According to Hindustani music theory, one octave contains twenty-two *shruti*s.

sur: note or tone.

***taan* (*tān*)**: fast note patterns in various arrangements, performed in both vocal and instrumental music. Typically performed at various moments of climax in a performance.

***talim* (*tālīm*)**: term for the process of training.

***taal* (*tāl*)**: rhythmic cycle comprised of a fixed number of beats.

***thumri* (*ṭhumrī*):** genre of composition and style of singing rooted in poetry that often revolves around romance and longing. Within its structure, it is known for lyrical expressiveness, specific use of musical ornaments, and melodic flexibility as compared to *khayal*.

***theka* (*ṭhekā*):** specific set of rhythmic syllables correlating with a specific taal. These string of syllables form the identity of the taal.

***upaj*:** akin to improvisation, referring to the spontaneous emergence of creative musical ideas, often associated with the simultaneous interweaving of taal, lyrics, and raag with an element of surprise.

***vistar* (*vistār*):** the process of exploration. In vocal and melodic instrumental music, referring to improvising in the framework of raag; in tabla, to the exploration of the taal.

A SONIC EXTENSION OF THEIR STORIES AND VOICES

Scan the QR code to listen to a curated playlist carrying music by the artists featured in the book.